D1826377

Cover art:

Front cover:
"Mandelbrot image"; Original created by "Chuculele" and released under *Creative Commons Attribution-Share Alike 3.0 Unported licence* (*CC BY-SA 3.0*). Reusable with attribution.

Rear cover:
Optical illusion images: released by original creators under Creative Commons CC0 Licence.
Man (Dale Bewan) with LSD blotters on tongue: Copyright © 2009 Dale Bewan.
Square of LSD blotter: Photograph of image released in to public domain by creator.

Complete cover image hereby released under *Creative Commons Attribution-Share Alike 3.0 Unported licence* (CC BY-SA 3.0).

Table of Contents

For my stepfather, who taught me to challenge assumptions and think for myself.

Foreword

"Be open to moments of true contentment and closeness with the universe. Look for them; don't bury that opportunity in the surface stuff like squiggly walls. Try to find open sky and look up at it; that is almost always the moment I feel most touched by the universe. Other people with more religious leanings would declare it like meeting God."

"Sebastian"

This is a book about self-discovery. It is also a book about LSD. It attempts to help you come to understand the important things you should know the first time you have a real trip with a psychedelic substance and how to get the most out of it rather than it being purely an experience of being 'high on a drug'. It really doesn't matter if you've tried other drugs before or even if you're a somewhat regular 'trashbag' that is more than familiar with a range of different substances; having a real trip on LSD or other psychedelics is going to be something new and different for you.

This book focuses on LSD, however could also offer valuable insights to a lesser degree for psilocybin (magic mushrooms), mescaline, DMT, 2CB, ibogaine and so on. That is not to say they are all the same – they are most certainly not; however the psychedelic experience and associated discovery of self can occur to at least some extent on any psychedelic substance, with LSD being the most likely to produce a profound and insightful experience.

First things first: A real trip will almost certainly change you. There is 'you before the trip' and 'you after the trip'. You can never go back. But – don't fear! – the 'you after the trip' is almost certainly going to be a better person in many ways than 'you before the trip' was. There are those who say they enjoyed it, but don't really think it changed them, only to find that sometime later, they're thinking about something and relate it to a revelation they had while tripping, giving them a new insight in to the problem that they might otherwise have missed. There are also those who take LSD but do not experience a 'trip' due to the circumstances in which they take it, or combination with other substances.

A trip is called so for a reason. It's not like going out and having fun using a substance to assist (as with amphetamines); or taking something filling your body with pleasure (like opiates). Instead it is a real journey – emotionally, possibly spiritually, most definitely psychologically, and often even physically (I will talk more about 'wandering around' later). It can be extremely enjoyable, and you can have a lot of fun. Nevertheless, it can also be harrowing, dark and scary. It can often be both good and bad alternately within a short space of time, and sometimes even – paradoxically – simultaneously.

In the pages of this book, you will find stories of trips that were taken; a detailed description of each part of the trip; and helpful information to make the most of the experience whilst avoiding some of the less helpful negative possibilities.

I hope that by the time you finish this book, you will truly understand why the LSD experience is called a 'trip' and – importantly – how to get out of the experience the most value for yourself possible.

It is possible that you are reading this book because you are interested in the substance and are considering trying it. It is also possible that you are extremely against 'drug use' and are shocked that anyone could write a book about the positive uses of a substance like LSD. Regardless of who you are and what preconceptions you are coming to this book with, I ask that you keep an open mind. Scepticism is good, as it helps you question what you read instead of accepting everything here without further evidence – but scepticism does still mean that *do* you question it, and not just outright reject it without further investigation.

The beginnings of this book were as a relatively humble six page 'leaflet' that I wrote for a friend of friend as she was interested in having her first LSD experience. As I wrote it, I thought to myself about the many things that could be added to it and expanded upon. Sometime later, I added a little more and as I did, the idea to turn it in to a complete book came to mind and I realised quite quickly that there was more than enough material in my head to do so.

I have done my best to take a fair and even approach to the psychedelic experience; however, I will not claim to be unbiased. No one is truly unbiased on this topic anyway. Either you have never tried it and can not speak from personal experience (often such people that try to talk on the topic have an agenda they are pushing) or you have tried it in which case your opinion is biased by your experiences. So yes, I am biased and I will freely state here that I believe the psychedelic experience to be a positive and good thing that – with the right direction – can be used to improve individuals' understandings of themselves and as a consequence humanity as a whole.

Nevertheless, in this book I talk about both the good and the bad. You will read about negative experiences and positive ones. I don't deny the existence of strongly negative experiences (so called 'bad trips') but now – after so many trips of my own – I believe I know how to avoid such experiences to a certain degree and will do my best to impart this knowledge to you. Even when having a strongly negative experience, it is also possible to gain positive things from it. I cover this and many such other points around this topic throughout the pages of this book.

As with most authors, I had some valuable help, without which I could not have completed this book. I want to thank my close friends that I have tripped with – Sebastian, Peter, and

George – both for the experiences they were a part of and for their valuable feedback on early drafts of the book. I want to thank Professor Doctor Torsten Passie PhD for taking the time to talk to me and provide me with valuable insights from the point of view of a both a medical professional and psychedelic explorer. I want to thank Doctor Melissa Barry PhD for her time taken to answer some of my questions about brain function. I want to thank Linnae Ponté from MAPS[1] for providing some information about psychedelic harm reduction in festival environments. And I want to especially thank my lovely wife Lindsay, who sat by my side documenting my behaviour, my ramblings and her own thoughts about me while I was tripping as a part of the research for this book, as well as having her own first ever psychedelic experience during (and influenced by) the writing of this book.

---

[1] Multidisciplinary Association for Psychedelic Research

About the Author

"I refuse to wake up one day, realise that I'm sixty years old and have spent the last twenty-five to thirty years doing nothing of any interest that I can look back on and remember as being of true value to myself. My thirty-four years so far have been a rollercoaster ride - lots of dizzying highs, lots of crushing lows. I regret none of it and will continue until my last breath."

"Dale Bewan"

So, who am I to be able to dispense this information to you? What makes me qualified to talk about LSD, psychedelic experiences and self-discovery?

My name is Dale[1]. I have taken LSD several hundreds of times in my life and many other psychedelic substances tens of times each. I have introduced people – including my wife – to LSD and (reasonably quietly for the most part) campaign for a greater understanding of this substance and enhanced states of mind in general.

Professionally, I am a software developer and I attribute a large amount of the creativity I have in my job to my usage of LSD. The things I have thought of while tripping, or later when referring back to trips have helped me become someone that understands both the technical and creative processes involved in software development; and execute on that understanding. It has also offered me insights in to how other people may perceive things and how I can use this to improve my software instead of only creating something that is tailored to my own way of thinking and desires.

In my private life, I am a married man and a father of one. My daughter means the world to me. She is two years old as I write these words and is highly intelligent which I am actively encouraging as much as I can. She is my pride and joy and I count her as the greatest blessing to have entered my life.

---

[1] My name is not Dale, but my wife (whose name is not Lindsay) insisted that I use a pseudonym when publishing this book as she has concerns that her family may come across it and not understand.

People are often shocked to hear that as a father I take LSD. They ask me how I can "do that to my daughter". The question stems from a false understanding of the situation. They hear 'father that uses drugs' and immediately a picture of a spaced-out 'Deadbeat Dad' enters their mind. If this thought entered your head as well, I hope the rest of this book will help you to consider differently. I don't consider myself a bad father for using LSD from time to time – on the contrary, I consider the ways in which LSD has improved my life to be aspects of myself that make me a better father than I would have been had I never taken LSD. I am more responsible, more accepting and can better shape my frame of mind to understand my daughter's needs.

Even aside from the many positives, a responsible LSD user trips far less often than many people go out and get drunk; and the next day, they are not a wreck like they would be if they were hung-over.

I never take LSD or any other substances in the presence of my daughter. This is not for fear that anything bad might happen (as you will read later, you do not 'lose control' under the influence of LSD) – but rather for the fact that me being in the psychedelic state of mind is likely to confuse and scare her somewhat with the many 'strange things' I might say or do.

My wife, Lindsay, had never taken LSD or any other illegal drug prior to meeting me. She had consumed alcohol, but only rarely and almost always in moderation. She is one of the many people that grew up hearing "drugs are bad" without ever being told that different drugs have different effects or that the only real distinction between the 'good drugs' from a doctor and the 'bad drugs' is a legal one and not based in any real way on scientific information.

Since knowing me of course, she has slowly begun to change her mind. At first, she would only accept my use of it if I were away somewhere else. After a while, she – perhaps out of curiosity – stayed with me as I took LSD at home and saw how it affected me. After some time, she also expressed an interest in using it one day in order to get a better understanding of herself – and importantly for her, a better understanding of me and why the topic is so important to me – but was naturally somewhat scared of the idea given her relatively reserved background and upbringing.

As I was writing this book, I had the great pleasure of being able to help Lindsay with her first LSD trip, which was a truly interesting and marvellous experience for her, as well as giving her the chance to learn more about herself. She has since expressed a desire to try it again, with a higher dosage next time, as the trip itself was quite mild compared to what I had described to her from my own experiences.

I was born in New Zealand, but have travelled the world extensively and lived in many countries. Lindsay is German and has never lived outside of Germany, but has travelled a little. Our backgrounds are very different, but we complement each other well and our differences make for interesting comparisons both with and without LSD.

I have Asperger's Syndrome. This is a topic that in and of itself could fill an entire book, but it is not the purpose of this book, so I will try to avoiding spending too much time on the topic. Suffice to say, Asperger's is a condition on the autistic spectrum and it means that in general, the way that I think about things and react to external stimuli is a somewhat different to the way that most other people do. There are many facets of the condition, but one very noticeable one is that I do not instinctually or natural recognise faces nor do I have any natural recognition for the emotions of others – I had to learn to 'read' a person's face in the same way that everyone else learns to read text on a page. Because of my Asperger's, I do think that LSD and other psychedelic substances probably do affect me a little differently than they affect other people, and it would be unfair of me to write this book and not explain that consideration.

A lot of my interest in LSD came from my condition, as I find LSD makes me in many ways closer to a 'neurotypical' mind when it comes to subjects like empathy and consideration of others[1]. However, this book was not written entirely from my own point of view – the experiences that I describe include both my own and those of others which I have learned from discussing the experiences at length.

I am sure there are experiences that I have had that are unique to people with Asperger's. Overall, these have been extremely positive and helpful for me, but I have taken care not to detail these within the pages of this book except where it is clearly noted that it is my own experience and not to be taken as an indicator of what you may experience. Therefore, despite my Asperger's syndrome, I feel the pages of this book are relevant for anyone whether they have a condition such as Asperger's or not.

I am not religious – and in some cases am even quite an outspoken atheist – although psychedelics have provided me

---

[1] Of course, the experience of LSD goes well beyond those simple facets and there is no way I would consider my mind 'normal' by any measure when having a psychedelic experience.

many opportunities where I have marvelled at the universe and indeed felt the existence of a presence, purpose or even 'grand scheme'. Religious people may interpret this as feeling closer to their deity or deities and people unsure of their beliefs may use it either as a justification to strengthen their beliefs or to discard them based on what they have learned.

I personally have never developed any religious beliefs, despite the feelings that I have had on psychedelics. I am a scientific minded person and find the ideas of belief without evidence and belief that can not change to be abhorrent concepts. I mention this here because throughout this book I will say only little about religion and will not speak in religious or mystical terms for the most part – it's simply not a factor in my thoughts most of the time whether I've taken LSD or not. This lack of a mention or my lack of faith should not discourage you from the book or the experience if you are a believer or follower of any particular religion – I just hope we can agree to disagree on our beliefs and leave it at that.

I am a passionately curious person. This in itself is probably the reason above all else that I developed such an interest in the psychedelic experience. I crave understanding in everything I come across and as such have interests that cover such diverse topics as historical linguistics, sociology, quantum physics, astrophysics, and – of course – psychopharmacology.

Once, under the influence of LSD, I formed an idea that others have called religious, although I would hesitate to do so. I postulated that given certain assumptions about the universe that may or may not be true according to our current scientific understanding, that all things that could conceivably come to pass must eventually do so. This includes the re-formation of structures that contain a consciousness that can be defined as 'you' including all of your own memories well after your death. Note that I do not actually necessarily believe this to be true, simply that if the assumptions are true, it is a logical conclusion. It is based on three assumptions that have not yet been definitively scientifically proven one way or another. If you are interested in this idea, you can read the details in the chapter titled "LSD and Creativity".

The Effects of LSD

"I think LSD changes everybody. It certainly makes you look at things differently. It makes you look at yourself and your feelings and emotions. And it brought me closer to nature, in a way – the force of nature and its beauty. You realize it's not just a tree; it's a living thing. My outlook certainly changed – and you dress differently, too!"

Ringo Starr

Will you still be in control of yourself under the influence of LSD? Will you go off and do crazy things that will get you in to trouble? Dangerous things? Will you remember it the next day?

The answers to these questions are: yes; maybe; very unlikely; yes.

Under LSD you lose no control over who you are and very little over how you behave. You can still think – for the most part – rationally and clearly. However, the world is now different. It has become strange and alien. This can in some ways make you seem out of control – even to yourself – as you may no longer be able to react to the world as you would normally. However, with a typical dose as advised in this book, you will likely retain enough understanding of the world to be able to maintain a somewhat 'normal' aspect and full control if you absolutely must. Only with significantly higher doses do you start to enter the territory of 'losing all reality'.

But the world is now – as said – strange and alien, and you will almost certainly want to explore it if you are the curious type. Once you have become accustomed to LSD after many trips, you will probably be able to take a trip and stay at home 'enjoying your own brain'; however on your first trip (and many more after), it is very likely you will almost be compelled to go out and experience this strange new world. Even once you are more familiar to it, going out is usually far more preferable than sitting around at home.

But, to reiterate, you lose no true control over yourself. And you **will** remember everything clearly. Perhaps even more clearly than other events in your life due to the significance the trip may have had to you.

One of the first things to know about LSD is that it is going to change how you perceive the world. A good friend of mine that we will call Sebastian once said, "*Most drugs make you fucked up in a normal world; LSD makes you normal in a fucked up world*".

The core reason for this can be described as a breaking down of your natural filters. Everything you see, hear, taste and feel in normal life[1] is passed through a kind of filtering system in your brain. These filters have evolved over the millennia to help us determine what is 'important' and not overload us with 'unimportant' information – if our distant ancestors were being charged at by an angry mammoth, they did not want to stop to admire the pretty flowers (or more precisely, those who did were unlikely to pass on their genes further)[2].

LSD breaks down these filters. No longer do they stop you noticing things, or make you decide that certain things have less significance than others. This means that it is like you are a child again – everything you sense is new, and you are sensing it for the first time. You will probably discover – quite by accident – that there are some things you really love that you never knew of before. For me personally, one of the best experiences I discovered is drinking a glass of plain fizzy lemonade (for example Sprite™) and feeling the carbon dioxide bubbles on my

---

[1] Interestingly, smell is one sense that is used directly and is not 'filtered' like the other senses. Because of this, LSD generally has no effect on your sense of smell.

[2] Honestly, this is not a really a statement of reality and should be considered a cute analogy only – in reality, the filters evolved significantly before our ancestors were hunting mammoths.

tongue. Another such experience for me is the feel of the soft wool or cotton of fluffy towels or similar. You may enjoy these same things or you may enjoy totally different things. Chances are however, you will find something that is 'surprisingly good' for you that you had never previously paid much or any attention to at all.

Another – perhaps more technically precise – way of explaining these filters is that your brain has evolved to apply concepts to sensory input. The sensory input comes from your sensory organs (eyes, ears, skin and so on) to your brain's thalamus. Normally, information is then taken from the frontal cortex to apply a 'concept' to this sensory data. Once the concept is applied, the sensory data itself is ignored or thrown away and only the concept itself is processed. You have the concept and so no longer need the raw data itself.

You can actually test this yourself easily right now – assuming you're not some kind of car fanatic, go out to the street and look briefly at a car driving past.

Do that now, before you read any further.

Once you have come back, you will know what you saw and feel you have a good idea what it was. That seems obvious. But (assuming you didn't cheat and read this first), can you remember what the hubcaps were like? Can you remember whether the bonnet had a raised part in the middle or not? And if so, was it divided in to two parts by a divider in the middle or not? Can you remember if it had one exhaust pipe or more? What about the clothes the driver was wearing (assuming that he or she entered your field of vision)? These details were not important to you. You applied the concept of 'car' to the sensory input that you received – probably with some degree of 'metadata', such as the colour, general size, maybe the make and model if you're familiar with it, and so on – but the details aren't something you were expecting to need, despite your eyes having seen those equally as well as the things you did take note of; and so this additional sensory input, despite being as clear as any other, was discarded.

This is what LSD changes – the application of the concept to the raw sensory data is not done. This therefore allows you to deal with the raw data directly, without any preconceived ideas about what it might mean. Assuming you have not taken a massive dose, and subsequently 'lost all reality', you are still usually somewhat able to manually apply the concepts as needed, however it is no longer an automatic process in your brain. You can take in and truly appreciate the full input of your senses without any of it being discarded prior to your conscious mind gaining access.

In addition and complementary to this, you are now able to process significantly more of the input that you receive. Without your brain applying concepts to the input, you have provided a shortcut to the processing, giving more room for your brain to deal with a greater load of information in general.

Your brain receives around eleven million bits per second of sensory information coming in from your various sense organs; however, your conscious mind can only process around a maximum of two hundred bits per second (with fifty being a common estimate). In his book "The Doors of Perception", the author Aldous Huxley likened this function of the brain to the concept of a reducing valve. When you take a psychedelic substance, the effectiveness of this 'reducing valve' is limited – you open yourself up to the opportunity to process a much greater amount of the raw sensory data, even if it is sometimes more unstructured and difficult to focus on just one thing.

It is not uncommon to become for a while what my friends and I sometimes refer to as a 'sensation whore'; where everything you come across, you want to experience for the first real time. This is not something to be concerned about, but rather revelled in. The opportunity to experience tens of thousands of 'new things' in the space of only a few hours is something that most of us haven't had since we were newborn babies – seeing, hearing, touching and tasting the world around us for the very first time. Sadly, most of us do not have memories that go back that far in our own lives.

As an important note – this feeling will mostly disappear after the end of the trip; however, there is a reasonable chance that it will **never** disappear **completely** for the rest of your life. You are likely to find yourself being 'more aware' of everything forevermore. Again however, this is nothing to fear or be worried about – it is far more of a positive effect than a negative one. It is also – as far as we can tell – not a physical change of any kind in the brain, but rather a state of mind. Quite simply that after you have been in a state where you no longer filter things out from your mind, you are quite simply more open to doing this in everyday life.

Another sensory effect that can occur is synæsthesia. Synæsthesia is – roughly speaking – when the brain uses the wrong processing pathways in order to process a known input message. Natural synæsthesia is not altogether uncommon; however, for many people that experience it, they do not consciously pay attention to it. A common example is that of numbers having particular feelings associated with them. Seven is happy; thirty-two is sad; eighty-five is angry; and so on. While this kind of synæsthesia can occur on LSD, it is infrequent and also extremely easy to overlook or ignore with the myriad of other feelings being experienced.

The more common variety of synæsthesia – both with and without LSD – is the mixing of the basic senses. With higher doses of LSD (border-line on the dosage recommended in this book, so it may or may not occur for you on your first trip if following my recommendations), the most common effects in descending order are: 'seeing sounds' where sounds generate visual responses (usually flashes or pulses of colour); 'tasting light' where bright lights create bad tastes in the mouth (and some colours have specific tastes); and 'hearing touch' where physical contact with something generates an auditory response (quiet rasping sounds are often reported).

The breaking down of the filters also allows you to do some things that are actually impossible without the use of LSD. These things are not illusory or imagined, but in fact very real.

For example: in human vision, the light receptors of the eye are divided in to two kinds – 'rods', which are very sensitive, but can not see colour; and 'cones', which see colour but are much less sensitive. Because of this division, in low-light situations we are normally unable to see colour. Of course, the cones do still pick up very minute amounts of colour information, but this is then discarded by the filters in the brain as being 'unnecessary', trusting instead to the much more functional and powerful (but black and white) rods. With the filtering gone, your ability to determine the colour of things in moderate darkness is not removed.

When talking about LSD or substances with similar effects I much prefer to use the term 'psychedelic' (meaning: "*mind-*

manifesting") or 'entheogen' (meaning: *"creates the divine within"* [1]) to the word 'hallucinogen' (meaning: *"creates hallucinations"*).

The reason for this is that the word 'hallucination' implies something to many people that is ***not*** going to happen on an LSD trip. You will ***not*** see complete things that are not there and be unable to distinguish the fantasy from reality. You will not experience a giant bug walking down the street where no bug really exists. You will not think you have magic powers such as the ability to fly. You most definitely will not think you are a glass of orange juice and be afraid that someone will drink or spill you. These are fairly common myths that you may have heard yourself, but they are no more than that – myths.

There are in fact some substances that can produce these kind of hallucinations (along with other powerful deliriant effects) such as 3-Quinuclidinyl benzilate (commonly called 'BZ'[2]); however these kinds of substances are extraordinarily unpleasant, unhelpful and serve no place in a book about self-discovery or even one about recreational drugs in general.

That is not to say that LSD doesn't have some powerful effects on the basic senses. After all, the expectation of hallucinations has to come from somewhere. LSD in the right

---

[1] This can also be translated as 'creates God within', depending on the translator's choice for the root 'theo', also seen in words like 'theology' and 'theocracy'.

[2] Not to be confused with 'BZP' (benzylpiperazine), which is a recreational drug with similar effects to some amphetamines or a 'mild' ecstasy dose.

dose can have quite powerful effects on your basic senses even beyond the synæsthesia described above. The most common effects are visual; however auditory, tactile and other effects are well within the realm of possibility.

The visual effects can be quite varied. By far the most commonly reported visual effect is a kind of additional movement – one that causes otherwise still objects to appear to be infused with a life of their own where they pulsate or gently change shape in ways that are difficult to define.

This 'movement' effect can additionally provide more complex effects on objects that are not so simple. Stucco walls are a personal favourite of mine for this due to the many small bumps, ridges and so on. It can at times appear that there is an additional 'layer' added on top of the wall that is shifting – possibly in one direction or perhaps in patterns – over top of the more static wall below it.

Another common effect is that the amount of light given off by or reflected by objects may appear to vary over time; where a dark night sky that you stare at becomes brighter and brighter until it is almost like day – until you blink, and it is dark again[1]. This same effect can also appear on other objects, causing them to appear to glow.

These effects combined can at times cause objects to take on the appearance of other substances. A recent experience of mine

---

[1] This effect is actually slightly physical as well as mental; as dilated pupils is a common physical effect of LSD, so more light is in fact reaching your retina.

was that a large stone building I was heading towards appeared to be made entirely of plasticine, with the illusion persisting from a significant distance away right up until I arrived at it, reached my hand to the wall and touched it to feel the rough stone as it really was.

One visual effect that is significantly more difficult to describe is alterations to the 'amount of dimensionality' of the world. Objects, environments or other things may appear to be 'flat' despite not being so; or conversely, flat objects such as pictures may appear to have true depth. In some cases, the even more indescribable effect of being 'more three dimensional than normal' can occur, whereby everything just seems to stand out more from everything else than it normally would – and contrary to normal reason, with none of it being made 'less noticeable' by the virtue of other objects being 'more noticeable'.

Less common on low to moderate doses, but more common on higher doses are 'light show' visual effects. This is when light effects appear as sparks, lines or so on either on objects that are otherwise unlit or solidly lit; or simply in the air in front of your vision. The 'sparks' are not dissimilar to the effect you get when you 'see stars' from rubbing your eyes when you wake up in the morning[1], but significantly more pronounced, usually lower in quantity, much more colourful, and not necessarily moving in the same kind of ways. The 'lines' may simply be single lines, or may form geometric patterns – usually depending on your own frame of mind.

---

[1] Called "phosphenes"

Sadly, I do not think it is possible to accurately describe all of these visual effects beyond my meagre attempt here simply because the language that we use was built for the 'normal' world and not for the 'altered' world that one experiences on an LSD trip.

At the very least, the basic 'movement' effect that I described can be somewhat simulated by certain kinds of optical illusions. The cover of this book presents an example of this kind of illusion, where if you stare at the Mandelbrot (black splodge) in the middle of image, the multi-coloured 'tubes' leading to it will appear to be moving in some undefinable way. This kind of optical illusion is close (but not identical) to the kind of movement that you may see during a trip.

There are many similar optical illusions that should also provide the same – or at least similar – kinds of visual effect and should be relatively simple to find with a targeted web search.

Similar visual effects on otherwise truly inanimate objects can be experienced by watching certain videos and then looking away towards something in your near field of vision. Many such online videos suggest for you to look down at your keyboard after watching it, but any moderately patterned object in your near field of vision should work equally as well. Note that the video itself is not an example of the kind of effect you see on LSD; it is instead simply something that forces your perception to be altered briefly so the 'LSD effect' is what you see afterwards.

Such videos are available on YouTube™ or other video sharing sites simply by searching for "LSD effect" or similar.

One good example I have found at the time of writing is at: *http://www.youtube.com/watch?v=bB08ai6ub7w*

Note of course however that as with the optical illusions the effect is purely visual, containing none of the 'feel' of LSD, lasts only a few seconds after the video ends, and itself is extremely mild compared to what you are in for on an LSD trip.

All of the visual effects experienced on an LSD trip combined with the drastically altered way of thinking about things can – at times – produce something than might be likened to the traditional understanding of a hallucination. Later when you read about the story of my friend Sebastian's first trip, you will read that he experienced a 'goddess' looking down at him from the sky.

This kind of hallucination is the closest to what people think about when they hear the word, however still has some significant differences. No matter how much LSD you have had, you will be aware that it is not real – it doesn't appear to you in the same way as reality and is quite clearly something that is in your mind. Basically speaking, it's not dissimilar to when you look at clouds and see particular shapes – they're still just clouds, and you know it, but you can also say, "*that's a dog*", "*that's a train*" and so on. The difference to this 'imagination' is that when you do this looking at clouds, you usually consciously control it and look for patterns; whereas when you're experiencing an LSD trip, it often happens undirected and automatically.

Another sensory effect that is worth noting is a strong influence on another sense that most people are not aware of and is almost never listed along with the classic 'five' senses –

your sense of chronoception – that is, your inbuilt ability to measure time. LSD will strongly affect this sense.

A typical trip lasts up to twelve hours, with the most profound and powerful effects between around hour two and hour five, with significant effects continuing to around hour six. After these four hours, you will often feel a week has passed. The most likely explanation for this is simply the amount of sensory input that you are receiving causes your brain to assume that a great deal more time must have passed than is truly the case.

Another possibility is the state of heightened awareness may trigger a similar reaction to that of stressful situations as with the feeling that time 'slows down' when you're in a car accident, watching your child fall off a swing and hurt themselves, or so on. It is likely that both of these explanations play a role in this effect to an extent.

Interestingly not all senses are altered by LSD. The classic five other than smell, as well as chronoception and occasionally thermoception (sense of heat) most certainly are. However, your sense of proprioception (body location), equilibrioception (balance and acceleration) and nociception (pain) are generally completely unaltered.

Despite all of these sensory changes however, the 'primary' effect of LSD is that of changes to internal sensation and thought patterns as mentioned previously. The external sensory ('hallucinatory') effects, while sometimes quite powerful and often extremely enjoyable, should be considered secondary to the effects on internal sensation and patterns of thought.

This really is one of the defining points of a trip being used for self-discovery rather than simply to 'get high', in which the user often does their best to ignore or even block out the changed thought patterns and concentrate only on enjoying the 'pretty visual effects'.

An interesting note is that some effects are modified by both your changed state of mind and the visual distortions working together.

One such effect that often shocks many people is getting a glimpse of themselves in a mirror. Your brain is very well used to the sight of yourself in a mirror, and so it can be quite a shock for it to see something that is just a little 'different' to what it was expecting. Many people report considering their reflection to seem alien or strange – more so even than how they perceive other people, even those that they know well.

A word of warning with mirrors: If you find yourself disgusted by what you see, look away and put it out of your mind as quickly as you can. Many people can not handle seeing themselves so differently and any kind of panic that this causes could potentially ruin your trip for some time. If however you just find it 'interesting' instead, then I invite you to spend some time examining it. You will probably see yourself in a new light next time you look after the trip has ended.

Music is another interesting experience on LSD, although almost always extremely positive with no negative stories of the effects of music on a trip having being found during my research. The synæsthesia that you may experience can often allow you to see the music before your eyes – often very beautiful and may consist of distinct shapes or lines, or may be simple coloured patches or overlays on your vision.

Even without considering synæsthesia however, music can be a very wonderful experience. Parts of your mind are acting much more quickly than normal and you are able to process sensory information in much more detail than normal. This means that with music or other advanced complex patterns of sound, you have time to savour each individual note or sound, take it in fully for your examination and appreciation, and then move on to the next.

If you try this kind of music analysis without LSD, you'll usually find the music carries on too quickly for you to follow, forcing you to rely on your imperfect memory, which is less than satisfying when you've become familiar with the LSD enhanced method.

For me, the most interesting music when on LSD tends to be electronic music, and the least interesting is simple guitar, drums and keyboard with vocals over it (large subsets of which, I do greatly enjoy when not on LSD). There is a lot of complexity in electronic music that I find can only be truly appreciated when my mind is in a state ready to handle such complexity.

Sex on LSD is usually possible and can be extremely pleasurable, however generally on lower dosages only if you intend for it to be manageable through to completion. During my own LSD experiences, for a long time there was no way I could imagine being okay with the concept of having sex. Any 'biological' act disgusted me to quite a large degree as I would picture in my head the various internal bodily processes involved in the act (whether it be sex, eating, or using the toilet) and it would disturb me on a fairly fundamental level.

Thankfully, over the last few years, my disgust for normal biological processes has waned and these days it does not bother me at all. I can't say if this is due to changes within myself or simply becoming more familiar with the LSD experience, but I know that for some people, there is a similar level of distaste for these processes; and for others, there are no concerns at all right from the start.

Regardless of the reason for the disgust disappearing, it did. So, when my wife Lindsay offered the opportunity for my first time having sex while tripping, I could hardly say no – something new to experience is always a joy.

The biggest problem with sex on LSD is mental distractions. Both Lindsay and I had taken a small dose of LSD – enough for a very 'light' trip but not more – and I still found it difficult at times to concentrate on the task at hand.

My sexual arousal – both physical and mental – would wane very quickly any time there was any kind of pause, however would also quickly return when my mind went back to sex again. Overall, this was not unpleasant, as it made the sexual encounter last much longer than it might otherwise have.

Lindsay also experienced some difficulties with concentrating – as we were kissing, she would occasionally stop to laugh about things that were going on in her head, which in turn would distract me as well.

Due to the enhanced sensory perception, my skin was much more sensitive than normal. Unfortunately, Lindsay reported that hers was not. Nevertheless, we spent a lot of time experimenting with touch and we found that sensitive areas of my body – especially my nipples – would bring me to an almost orgasmic state without the necessity for actual physical arousal. At times, this was almost a kind of 'sensory overload' for me and

I had to stop her for a few seconds to recover and catch my breath.

Overall, I can highly recommend sex on LSD if the opportunity presents itself and the idea of doing so does not bother you, but be aware you might be in for a long and sometimes slightly confusing experience.

I have spent several pages on the effects of LSD on the mind, so what about effects on the body? Surely, there must be something to say about that?

As it turns out, there are surprisingly few physical effects. This is perhaps in part due to the very small amount of the substance being taken – as will be mentioned in more detail a little later, LSD is taken in quantities that are measured in 'tens of micrograms' rather than the more common 'tens of milligram' quantities for many (if not most) other recreational substances. That is to say, a thousand-fold smaller amount of substance. It seems likely that most physical reactions outside of the brain therefore simply are not getting enough of the substance to be noticeable.

It is, generally speaking, quite difficult to get an accurate picture of the physical effects, as many are potentially associated with psychological effects that in turn alter physical state. For example, if increased heart rate is recorded in someone who has taken LSD, is it an effect of the LSD, or is it an effect of what is going on in his or her mind? Just as when you are excited, in love, or scared your heart rate increases, so it may increase from these feelings occurring during an LSD trip.

One definite physical effect that is generally seen is pupil dilation. This tends to vary in intensity with different people and of course different amounts of LSD. In general, it is quite noticeable, however still somewhat less than is seen in people who have taken substances such as MDMA that are renowned for relatively extreme dilation.

Other effects often listen as physical effects include: wakefulness; appetite changes – usually 'much lower' to 'none at all' but occasionally higher appetite is seen; temperature changes – both up and down; and heart rate changes – usually up, but occasionally down. These apparent physical effects may however in reality all be secondary effects that are brought on by the primary psychological effects rather than being directly physical effects themselves.

Your First Trip

"The first time I had acid, a light bulb went on in my head and I began to have realizations which were not simply, "I think I'll do this," or "I think that must be because of that." The question and answer disappeared into each other. An illumination goes on inside: in ten minutes I lived a thousand years. My brain and my consciousness and my awareness were pushed so far out that the only way I could begin to describe it is like an astronaut on the moon, or in his space ship, looking back at the Earth. I was looking back to the Earth from my awareness."

George Harrison

The idea of 'Set and Setting' was first put forth by Doctor Timothy Leary, one of the pioneers of the use of psychedelic substances for exploration of the self and the mind.

Basically speaking, 'Set' is how you feel about yourself and your state of mind; and 'Setting' is the environment in which you're in, including the location, people, weather and other external factors. These two factors are the most important things under consideration for any psychedelic experience; and your first is no exception.

You should not be scared. That is a part of what this book is trying to do – assuage any fears you have so that you can get the most out of your trip. If you are scared, you may find the trip disturbing and horrid. But, good news! There is no such thing as a 'bad trip' as you have likely had it described to you. A trip certainly can have elements of being 'bad', but that can be turned around and fixed very easily – you're in control and it's up to you to do it. It is all a case of Set and Setting. For this reason, many people involved in psychedelic research prefer the term 'difficult experience' to 'bad trip' as it more accurately reflects the reality of the situation.

If you are in a bad place in your mind, having horrid experiences, tell your guide (more about him or her later) or any other friend familiar with LSD. They should be able to either distract you long enough that your unpleasant experiences will be nothing but a memory or perhaps even direct the negative thoughts towards a positive learning experience.

'Setting' is important, just as 'Set'. However, it is significantly easier to get the right setting. The most important part of getting the right setting is simply in knowing what to avoid.

Crowded areas full of strangers are best avoided. This includes both situations such as 'a shopping mall' as well as 'nightclubs'. While there are those that enjoy taking a small amount of LSD or combining it with a different substance and then going out to a nightclub, this is not the appropriate setting for a real trip. It can very easily lead to anxiety and panic as well as being an inappropriate environment for the kind of reflection and self-study that I emphasise throughout this book. If you are only interested in going out to 'party' on LSD, this book really is not for you.

Situations where you need to interact with people that are not aware you have taken LSD are also important to avoid. Some people have no difficulty in interacting with others whilst tripping, however the vast majority of people find it difficult, uncomfortable or distasteful.

A common mistake amongst smokers is to not take enough cigarettes with them and then need to purchase more at the height of the trip. Even the simple act of purchasing cigarettes may feel like a difficult proposition at this time. As an ex-smoker myself, I personally recommend taking around twice as many with you as you would consume on a 'heavy' night of smoking, such as when out drinking alcohol or similar. This is probably much more than you will actually need, but it is better to be safe than sorry.

After your first few trips, you may be more comfortable around people and can relax these restrictions slightly; this is up to you. However, to me, the best trips are always those with a small to medium number of friends in environments with a decent amount of nature around (the walkways around Bondi Beach in Sydney; the Eilenriede forest in Hannover; and so on).

Conversely to things to avoid, there are also certain things that will improve the setting in general. That is to say, the things that you **should do** for your first trip (and subsequent trips until you are comfortable with your own needs).

You should always have somewhere to go that is warm and comfortable. You do not need to spend the entire trip there – you might or might not – but if you are going out, you need to have this place to return to after you're done. It may be your home, given that there is no one else there who would react negatively to you on LSD; it may be a friend's house; or it may even be a hotel room. Regardless of where or what exactly it is, you should think of this place as your 'safe haven' and generally the trip will both begin and end in this location.

An extremely important point for your first trip (and many thereafter) is to take it with other people and not on your own. If you want to take it and no one else you know does, at least ask one or more people you trust to stay with you throughout the experience. If they are not willing to do so, **do not take the LSD**.

As described throughout this book, LSD itself is non-harmful; but there is no way to be sure what it is going to do you personally. Everyone's mind is different and therefore everyone's LSD experience is different. Taking it alone without significant prior experience may turn out fine, but it equally may turn out to be the most horrific experience of your life. At best for your first few times, you should take it with someone who can act as a 'guide' for you. This will be explained in more detail later.

While it may sound odd to mention, as a practical matter you should make sure you have eaten and used the toilet before the LSD begins to take effect. Some people experience a strong distaste of 'biological' matters (potentially including eating; sex; and going to the toilet) when tripping. You might not experience this particular distaste; but if you do, you will be glad you got the necessary things out the way beforehand.

You need to be aware that LSD takes some time for the effects to take hold. With the advised dosages given in this book, you will probably begin to feel some slight effects at around thirty minutes after taking it, but it may take up to an hour longer than that. Do not assume that nothing is happening or that the minor experiences you get at first are all that is going to happen and then be tempted to take more. Another thirty to ninety minutes after you begin to feel the first slight effects, you will begin experiencing the trip much more seriously. This is detailed further in the chapter "Structure of the Trip".

If you are going to be wandering around – which is quite likely, as you will read throughout this book – you should bring something to drink, as a lot of walking around – especially in warmer climates and seasons – can cause dehydration. The drink should be non-alcoholic and I recommend neutral flavours such as water or plain lemonade as you may find other flavours take on unusual aspects that you were not expecting.

Body weight does not play a strong role in determining the strength of a trip. You may have heard of people recommending dosage based on weight and indeed, I used to naïvely do so myself; however, it was pointed out to me by a medical researcher of LSD that this is generally not the best way to handle the dosage.

In general, every person has a specific 'constitution' for handling mind-altering substances and this is what should be taken in to account. The body weight is likely to play a role in your constitution but it is far from the primary determining factor. A simple – although possibly incorrect for some people – measure is to base it on your tolerance for alcohol. If you are a 'lightweight' that gets tipsy from one drink, you may find it takes only a small dose of LSD to have an effect. If you can drink 'quite a lot' without feeling any effects, you may need more.

For a 'good first trip', I generally advise in the range of 125μg (micrograms) at the lower end of the scale to around 250μg at the higher end. This is a relatively strong dose – a little higher than is used in most psychedelic research experiments, but quite a bit lower than the amount generally used in LSD assisted psychotherapy.

The type of mental state that you hold normally will also affect the amount that LSD influences you. If you are the kind of person who is very structured, organised, rigid, and so on, then you may find you will not allow your mind the freedom to fully experience a good trip at first. That is not to say it will not do anything, as with any reasonable dosage, the effects are quite impossible to ignore or fight against.

At first, it seems logical to assume that if you are a person who is uptight in this way, you should take a larger dose so that you are 'forced' in to the experience. This may work, however could also lead to significantly more panic and anxiety as you try to fight against it and fail. My advice in this case would be to take the LSD a bit at a time – starting with 100μg and then after ninety minutes taking another 50μg, with another 50μg every hour thereafter until you have taken the amount that is right for you. It may be that the initial 100μg 'loosens you up' enough that you do not need more, or it may be the case that a little more is needed. Note however that doing this will extend the overall length of the trip by some time and so you need to be prepared for this.

It is important to be careful with dosage, but not in the way you probably think. LSD is an extremely non-toxic substance. You could easily take twenty times my recommended amount with no harmful effects on your body (although I make no promises about harmful effects to your ego or sense of self with such a dosage).

What you need to beware of is taking too little. This will not be harmful of course, but it also will not give you the experience that LSD is capable of giving you. While this may not sound like such a bad thing, having a minor experience will not only be less helpful and useful to you, but as it is significantly 'easier' to manage, it may leave you expecting that a future stronger trip will be the same, causing it to be even more difficult and unpleasant.

There are generally two kinds of people who take LSD. One is the kind of people who take relatively small amounts to feel just the 'edges' of a trip and then go out to nightclubs and parties. They may also take a little more if they are combining it with other substances – almost all other substances will either lessen the effects of LSD or cause the trip to become unmanageable. Alcohol is the worst for this in my experience, rendering LSD quite impotent beyond some minor visual disturbances on top of the drunken state. Maybe you have done this or something similar yourself – if so, you have still never had a real LSD trip and should definitely continue reading this book as if you had never taken it before at all.

The other kind of people who take LSD are the people more like myself. These are the people who want to experience something totally new, every time – even after hundreds of trips. This group could be divided yet again in to groups such as the 'mystical' or 'spiritual' types and the 'scientific' or 'practical' types. However, this distinction is actually significantly less important and contains so much crossover that many – if not most – people would not fit neatly in to either group. The point is to take the new experiences and do something with them that fits to you – for the first type, this may be a kind of mystical revelation showing them new things about themselves or their beliefs; and for the other, it may be a betterment of their understanding of themselves and the universe we all inhabit. In reality, these are exactly the same thing – just two different ways of looking at it.

For your first trip, you **should** have a 'good strong trip' as described above. If you take too little, you won't just be 'tripping a bit less', you'll be missing out on a whole gamut of experiences that you could have, and may go away thinking of LSD experiences as something less profound than they really are. It may be 'fun', but it will be significantly less enlightening and useful to you than it might otherwise be.

To be fair, there are of course dosages that would be 'too much' for a first trip as well. The largest dose I ever took was somewhere around 600μg. This was quite an experience and not something I regret at all; however, I also would not recommend this to others until they are very experienced and sure of their own minds. For a time under this dose, I lost all sense of the real world and (lying on my floor without moving – as far as I know) spent an undefinable amount of time completely embedded in a fantasy world of my own making with no escape or even realisation that the real world outside of my mind continued to exist.

At one point during this 'loss of reality', I even experienced complete ego dissolution – that is to say, I no longer had a sense of self – I, quite simply, did not exist anymore from my point of view and words like "*I*", "*me*", and "*myself*" would have been meaningless to me had I in some way come across them. It was beautiful, wondrous, and enlightening – but also somewhat harrowing. I most certainly intend to repeat the experience, and maybe even higher doses, at some point when I am well prepared for it, however I can not imagine it being enjoyable nor at all helpful for a first time user.

Aldous Huxley described an incident under psychedelics where he experienced at least partial ego loss as follows: "*[I experienced] the direct, total awareness, from the inside, so to say, of Love as the primary and fundamental cosmic fact. ... I was this fact; or perhaps it would be more accurate to say that this fact occupied the place where I had been. ... And the things which had entirely filled my attention on that first occasion, I now perceived to be temptations - temptations to escape from the central reality into a false, or at least imperfect and partial Nirvanas of beauty and mere knowledge.*"

If you take the dosages recommended earlier, you are very unlikely to want to do LSD again immediately. If you did however, you should be aware that there is a significant tolerance build-up[1]. Taking the same amount again will have almost no effect for the next four to seven days. You could

---

[1] This tolerance build-up includes a cross-tolerance with many other psychedelic substances also. If you have just experienced an LSD trip, a typical dosage of psilocybin for example will also have significantly less effect than it normally would.

repeat the experience with a much higher dose, but I strongly recommend you do not do so. Instead, take the time to reflect on this trip and look forward to the next one at some point later in the future. I personally find that around two to three months is a good 'cool down' time between serious trips; and longer if the trip you experienced had strong negative aspects.

As mentioned, it is best to take your first LSD trip with someone that is experienced and capable of acting as a guide to help you get the most out of it. Later in this book, I talk about medical research of LSD, including in the realm of psychotherapy. In these cases, the researcher – a trained psychologist, psychiatrist or psychotherapist – is acting as a guide. In informal settings, the guide's job is similar, however their background and experience is likely quite different.

An unfortunate reality is that it is not always possible to have a guide available, as you may not know anyone meets the criteria to be your guide. In that case, make sure you are with good friends who will look after you and help you through any difficulties as a guide would. To make the most of the situation, I would advise that your friends also read this book before you embark on the trip.

If you are lucky enough to have a guide, there is a good chance that you are reading this book under their advisement. They will be able to tell you a lot more about their own experiences as well to complement what you read here. More importantly, they will also be able to tailor some information to you specifically, as the LSD experience takes a lot from 'who you are' which I of course can not cover in this book in any kind of full or detailed fashion.

It is also possible that you are reading this book out of interest only, being already very familiar with LSD. If that is the case, I encourage you to be a guide for others, and use the information provided here to get a good idea of what you should and should not do.

What are the properties that someone needs to have to be a good guide for you or that you need to have to be a good guide for others?

Your guide is a good friend of yours. You trust him or her as someone that will look after you when you are in trouble; as someone you can talk to about your feelings; and as someone that has your best interests at heart.

Your guide has taken LSD on several occasions in their past and understands the effects that it has on the psyche as well as the senses. In the best case, they have acted as a guide before, but of course, there is a first time for anything, so it is okay if they have not.

They will make sure you are properly prepared for your trip – both practically (as with items listed earlier in this chapter) and mentally.

The most important job of the guide however is to simply be with you during the trip; be ready to help you whenever you need it; and be ready to leave you to your own thoughts when you need that instead.

LSD can be either *terrific* or *terrible*. Note that the root of both of these words is the same – terror. LSD will push towards your limits and in some cases may push you over. It is the job of your guide to make sure that your trip is leaning towards *terrific* and not *terrible.* Either way however can be a positive experience for you if you let it.

Your guide may or may not take LSD with you. Generally speaking however, they will. This is something that surprises many people the first time, as they feel that if you are taking a drug, surely it must be best to have someone there that is not under the influence of it in case of any problems. With LSD, this is not so much of a concern. Your guide knows the experience and knows that they will be able to do anything they need to do to look after you while still tripping themselves. It is of course most likely that they will only take a 'moderate' dose of LSD – that is, similar to the dose that you yourself take – which for them is enough to have a good trip, but not enough for them to lose their grip on reality (you may well do so, and this is nothing to fear, but due to their experience, they will not).

It is also the case that when your guide takes LSD with you, they are themselves better prepared to help you in some ways. Having a like state of mind helps them to understand what you are experiencing in a way that someone not sharing the experience can never really do. In early medical research, as you will read later, it was common for researchers to experiment with the substance on themselves. They did this in order to understand it better, and in some earlier cases of LSD assisted psychotherapy before the world became used to such ideas being 'unthinkable', the psychotherapist would even use the substance during the session with the patient for the same reasons.

It is also for the 'like state of mind' reason that people who often trip with their close friends automatically start acting as guides for each other without having ever really planned to do so. This is certainly the case for me and my close friends – when necessary I will look after them and in turn, they will look after me.

The first thing that your guide will do with you after you have taken the LSD is talk to you as you wait for the trip to start coming on. During this phase, you can experience some minor anxiety and simple conversation about anything will help keep you distracted and put you in a good mood.

Once the trip itself begins, your guide will try to assess your state of mind and will act according to that.

If all is well, they will offer ideas for activities that you can do – most likely going for a walk through nature, or if you live in a place with beautiful architecture and not too many people around, some quiet streets. I will elaborate more on this in the next chapter.

If however you are having difficulty with the trip, your guide's job is instead to help guide your thoughts in more positive directions. This is best done in a reasonably quiet, safe feeling environment inside. Some light background music may be very helpful. They will talk to you about things likely not even related to the trip, and help get your mind to wander in the right direction.

It is important to realise that your guide is only human. They can not control what you are thinking or feeling; nor can they do anything to make the trip end earlier if you are uncomfortable with it. Your thoughts and feelings will be directed by yourself and your environment and your guide will make this as pleasant and as useful as possible, but it is up to you to make the most of what your environment is offering.

The most important thing for you to remember is to talk to your guide about your feelings. If they suggest you go out and you are not comfortable with doing so, **you must say so**. You do not need to feel like you are letting them down, or that you should somehow be obligated to follow their ideas. On the contrary, it is their job as the more experienced tripper to make sure that your trip is as good and as useful as it can be. They will listen to you and take direction from what you want to do.

As the trip begins to end, your guide will help smooth over some of the potentially uncomfortable feelings that can be associated with normalcy returning. Again, the main method they will use to do this is simply talking to you. If the situation permits it, they may offer to put on some kind of background to concentrate on such as television or music. If you would prefer to be left with your own thoughts however, tell your guide this, as the background noise or images may interfere with what can be a very beautiful – and useful – part of the trip.

Once the trip is completely over, your guide's job is almost done, but not quite. If you're up to it, they should talk to you about your experience, make mental or written notes for the next time you trip together (if there will be a next time) and then be better prepared to help make your next trip even more wonderful than this one was.

Overall, the guide's job is not very different from that of a psychotherapist using LSD as an aid in their therapy. Most likely however, your guide is not a trained psychotherapist and is instead relying on their own knowledge and understanding to help you get the most possible out of your psychedelic experience.

If you are interested in being a guide for others, I do recommend reading **at least** a little about philosophy, psychotherapy, states of consciousness, and other related topics. Some of these topics are covered within this book to a degree, but it would help a great deal to make use of further resources by people more knowledgeable than I am. It will be invaluable in helping you understand yourself, which is a pre-requisite to helping others understand themselves.

Structure of the Trip

"For a timeless moment, a reality is experienced that exposes a gleam of the transcendental reality, in which universe and self, sender and receiver, are one."

Albert Hofmann

While every trip will be a unique experience and generally progress almost completely unplanned as far as the details are concerned, it is possible to expect a rough structure or to plan to your general activities such as location, basic activities and so on based on the expected progression of the LSD's effects on you. For your initial trips, I recommend that these plans be made and agreed to by everyone involved before taking the substance. Once you are much more familiar with the experience, the process becomes more natural and less planning is needed, however at least some (location, weather-preparedness, etc.) is always advised.

Generally, for the information that I present to you in this chapter, I am making the assumption that you are taking LSD in the evening and experiencing the LSD trip at night.

There are many positive benefits to having the psychedelic experience in the day instead – such as not messing up your natural wake/sleep rhythms, and getting to see more of the natural beauty of the world – however for the majority of people, this isn't possible due to the number of distractions, number of unwanted people around, and so on.

If you do have the opportunity to take it in the day instead – and I can highly recommend doing so if the opportunity is available – then the progression of the effects will of course still follow this pattern; however any mentions that I make of tiredness and sleep will likely not apply and some additional caution may be needed in order to avoid crowds of people or certain kinds of dangerous situations.

The following time progression will be roughly what you can expect from a typical LSD experience.

1) Initially: Take LSD

2) 20 to 90 minutes later: Begin to feel the first effects and experience a 'ramping up' of the experience.

3) 40 to 60 minutes after feeling the first effects: Experience the full effects of the LSD – often simply called 'The Adventure'

4) 3 to 5 hours after the adventure started: Start to experience some 'moments of lucidity'

5) 90 minutes after the moments of lucidity first began to appear: The LSD is starting to wear off; this is 'chill out' time.

6) 2 to 2.5 hours after the start of 'chill out' time: The LSD has almost entirely worn off with only 'back of the mind' effects remaining for up to two more hours.

Each stage of the progression of course deserves a much more detailed description than this short list.

Take LSD

As described earlier in this book, it is strongly advised that for your first trip (and the vast majority thereafter) you take LSD with friends that you trust; and for your first several trips preferably at least one of which is already experienced with the substance to act as your guide.

It is sadly not always possible to follow this exactly, as you may not know anyone that has experienced it before – or at least, may not be aware that they have.

For your first trip – and indeed the best trips thereafter – I highly recommend that you are somewhere 'peaceful'. This could be at a good friend's house with nature nearby; at a quiet deserted beach or forest (if you are lucky enough to live in or near a location that has such things) that you know well; or similar. As you will read throughout this book, the experience more or less demands that your environment is one in which you can feel safe and secure; as well as being one in which you can explore both the world around you and within your own mind.

The actual act of taking LSD is not a complex process – it is pretty much exclusively taken orally and is as simple as eating something. The process is generally referred to as 'dropping acid', hence the title of this book. You can learn more about what the various delivery mechanisms of LSD look like and how you take it in the chapter "Where do I get it and how do I take it?"

It is of course – as with any other substance – technically possible to take LSD in other ways. The author Aldous Huxley, as he lay on his deathbed, asked his wife to inject him with 100µg of LSD intramuscularly. This should of course be considered a special case however, as he was fully aware of his impending death and he clearly wanted the effect to be as immediate and potent as possible. There is no reason that LSD would be injected under any normal circumstances. Outside of medical research and special cases such as Huxley's, I have never encountered LSD being used in this manner.

First effects and ramping up

At this stage, you are beginning to feel the first effects, however you are unsure if you are imagining it or not. This is in fact completely normal and is a sign that the LSD is beginning to take effect, even though you yourself would adamantly say you could not yet be certain of it.

Some introspection may begin taking place where you wonder how much you are able to actually influence your own feelings and whether you really can trick yourself in to thinking that you are tripping.

This kind of introspection is likely to increase over the course of the trip. Of course, after a while, you most certainly will 'realise' you are tripping – it will in fact become impossible to ignore it. That stage however is still yet to come and it is usually not a sudden occurrence, but rather one that you find has crept up on you without you being aware of it.

You may find yourself at times becoming a little confused at this point if you are not used to introspection. It can lead to circular reasoning that would normally be quite easy for you to resolve; but in your current state, you find yourself always coming back to the same points over and over.

This can be frustrating, as you feel that there is something really interesting you could discover or learn, but just can't quite get it. But, at this early stage of the trip, it is not likely to lead to anything further. You can be content in the thought that as the LSD begins to have a greater effect on you, solving these conundrums both becomes easier to do as well as – perhaps paradoxically – less important to you.

After a little while, you'll start to feel that you're not quite certain if you're tripping or not – you can no longer so definitely say that there's no way you're being influenced by the drug, but you also can't yet say that you're experiencing the 'trip'. It is not uncommon to feel some anxiety your first time at this stage as thoughts of the upcoming unknown experience go through your mind and the knowledge that there's nothing you can do to stop it.

This is normal behaviour of a rational mind in circumstances of expectation or anticipation of the unknown. It is not dissimilar to people's fears the first time they fly on a plane; or start their first day in a new job.

Try to let any anxiety out of your mind and enjoy the experience. Talk to your friends or your guide.

At this stage, it is very important that you are comfortable, as any bad feelings that you experience at this point are capable of shaping the rest of the trip if you let them. If you do have bad feelings, do not dwell on them or be concerned that the rest of the trip is going to be bad as well; you have the power to change things simply by putting it out of your mind and enjoying yourself.

Your company and environment are the best tools to allow you to enjoy this phase of the trip. Talking nonsense with your friends; listening to some background music; or even engaging in simple activities like watching a movie or playing Guitar Hero™ on the easiest setting are going to help you pass the time happily until the trip begins to take full effect.

Towards the end of this phase, and before the trip takes a strong hold, the 'visuals' will start to appear. These are the visual effects as described earlier in this book.

As the visuals begin to appear, you will likely find that if you were using simple activities to pass the time, your interest in them begins to wane, or they become more difficult to perform. The primary reasons for this are that you are beginning to experience a more 'whole' reality. Concentrating on a single task becomes undesirable as your mind begins to pay more attention to everything that is around you.

The visuals will begin as subtle shifts in perception. If you're inside, the room's dimensions may seem somehow 'different' – perhaps larger than before, perhaps smaller, perhaps just a different shape. You may begin to feel a little uncertain about moving around since now everything is just a little different than it was, but if you actually try, you will find you can manage it perfectly well – often to the point that you surprise yourself in your ability to do so.

After the shifts in perception, you will likely start to see the first bits of 'movement'. Curtains with folds in them, rough surfaces, or other complex patterned objects will be first. You will begin to see things starting to shift around. I truly can not describe this movement in any way that makes sense, because the movement itself does not. Things are moving, but they are also quite clearly staying still. If it were truly moving, the position of it would change – but the position remains fixed, while the movement is nevertheless there.

It is highly recommended to use the beginning stages of the visuals to accustom yourself to them during your first few trips. They are going to become significantly more powerful as time progresses. During these initial stages, you may even find you can 'turn them on and off' at will; however later they will be a constant companion until the trip begins to wind down towards the end. This is not something to be concerned about – in fact, it is one of the truly enjoyable parts of the experience if you allow it to be so. I've had so many strange and interesting visuals, which during the height of the trip have given me a very different perspective on things that I've been able to hold on to ever since.

The adventure

This is the start of the part that could be considered the main 'adventure' of the trip. Anything can (and most likely will) happen. There is no way I can tell you exactly what is going to happen, but it is going to be incredible – if you let it.

At this point, the visual and other sensory effects are impossible to ignore and are going to remain strong for quite some time; however you should not let them define the experience for you – there is a lot more happening 'inside' your mind at this point if you take the opportunity to allow yourself to experience it.

In my experience, around ninety percent of people want to go out and 'wander around' at this stage. This of course also changes depending on the environment available to wander around in, including of course the weather, time of day and number of people around.

If you do want to go out, you – with your guide and friends – definitely should do so. Wanting to go out but not doing so can lead to feelings of being 'cooped up' and can become unpleasant if not dealt with correctly.

At times however, you may find you can not go out for whatever reason. Maybe you are in a group and some members of the group do not want to, but you do. Or maybe you would like to, but it is twenty below zero and sleet is flying at a near ninety degree angle. Whatever the reason, you are going to need to deal with it in such a way that you still enjoy the experience and do not have a negative experience.

The best way to do this is simply to do all the same things you would do if you did not want to go out to begin with. In a reasonably short space of time, you will find that you can adjust your views and desires to suit the situation. And – as a bonus – once you have learned to do this effectively, you will be able to do it almost at will and make the most of any situation that presents itself from then on in.

Conversely, if you are not comfortable with the idea of braving the world outside, do not feel compelled to! Just because you are having an adventure, you do not need to actually go anywhere to do so. The adventure can take place within the confines of a single room if necessary.

As a general rule of thumb for groups – stay together. If one member of the group that has taken LSD does not want to go out, the group should not go out. As above, getting used to staying in is fine, but going out when you do not want to is only a recipe for disaster.

If your group is large enough, you can split in to sub-groups of no less than three people, as long as each sub-group contains at least one person that is relatively experienced with a trip to act as a temporary guide while the main guide of the trip is not with you.

If you are staying in, there are a lot of things you can do, but you will probably just find yourself talking to each other for a very long time. Bouncing ideas off each other as they come in to your mind; discussing the feelings or visual effects that you are experiencing; or even just light-heartedly joking or talking about common interests. If possible, I recommend some background music during this, but it is definitely not required – there's more than enough stimulation generated from within your own mind to really need any external stimuli at all.

A lot of people think that watching something 'trippy' on TV might be a good idea. Something like *"Fear and Loathing in Las Vegas"* or *"2001: A Space Odyssey"*. However, this actually turns out to be a bad idea most of the time. Movies direct you to follow a story; they have a progression (even if twisted sometimes) that is designed for a normal mind to follow. Your mind is not normal right now. You will likely find the story either difficult or uninteresting. The visual effects that you experience in the real world will be muted or removed on the screen; or you may experience a different kind of visual effect from the pixels (depending on the screen resolution and how close you are) that distracts from the film itself.

At the very best case, your mind will allow itself to be led by the movie, and for the duration of the movie, you will experience less of the trip than you might otherwise – effectively 'wasting' that time. This – in theory – could be helpful if you are having difficulty with the trip, however in practice it rarely works, as difficult trips are usually strong enough that your mind will not allow itself to be so easily brought back to any kind of reality.

If you must put something on the screen for whatever reason, the something like Disney's *"Fantasia"* might be a good choice. It has music that you can enjoy, bright colours, and movement to watch (but again, it will probably make the trip less interesting). But, most importantly, it has no storyline – it is purely something for the senses to take in without the need to follow a story idea from the start to the end.

It could be though that you do not want to just sit and talk. Depending on how much you took and how much it affects you as a person, it may be that you do not feel up to talking to others. This is okay too. If you are 'tripping hard' and can not really talk to people, signal this to others and they will steer away from talking to you. This is a time for you to enjoy something uniquely personal. Look in the direction of something patterned – a carpet, curtains, wallpaper, whatever. You do not need to concentrate to stare at it, just look and hold your gaze in that general direction. The visual effects will begin to shape themselves according to your thoughts. Just relax and watch them. You may find you can control their direction with your mind, or you may find you can not. Either way, they will begin to do things that will shape your thoughts in new ways. You will most likely begin to enter a kind of trance. Let this happen – **do not fight it**. When you are ready to come out of it, you will do so, and attempting to do so before you are really ready will only lead to negative feelings. This may last thirty seconds, or it may last several hours. Regardless of how long it really lasts, you will probably feel it lasted many times longer than it really did.

Something that can have a powerful influence on you at the start or end of this stage is music – as stated, it is certainly not required, but while the trip is not quite at its most intense, the stimuli provided by music can be extremely effective for directing your thoughts. Everyone has his or her own musical tastes, and so I can not tell you specifically what it is that you should listen to for the most enjoyment. However, as a general pointer, try to find music that contains a relatively high level of complexity and speed. My personal music tastes are quite wide ranging; covering many different styles including the likes of *The Beatles*, *The Cure*, *Brahms*, *Beethoven*, *Nine Inch Nails*, *IAMX*, *Howling Bells*, and *Sigur Rós* just to name a few bands and composers of some vastly different styles. Under the influence of LSD however, I tend to prefer more long electronic sounds as found in various kinds of dance or trance music – but most especially the styles appropriately called 'Acid Trance', 'Psychedelic Trance' and similar. The track *"Halcyon + on + on"* by *Orbital* epitomises this kind of music for me and continues to be a favourite of mine whilst tripping in a more relaxed state. In some other states of mind however, I do prefer something faster that gives me more input to process.

The reason that music can be so powerful is your changed perception and ability to focus more finely on specific details combined with a distorted sense of time. At the height of a good trip, it is possible to take each sound made by the music as an individual and unique experience, savour it, analyse it at your leisure and then move to the next. At the same time, you can take a full several minutes of music as one individual part and examine your feelings about that simultaneously with each small sound.

Quite simply, when you are tripping and in a situation where listening to music is possible, I recommend you try out various different styles and see what suits you best. Tastes in music are varied, as is the LSD experience, however if you appreciate music at all, I am quite certain that you will find the appreciation enhanced by the experience.

A good friend of mine related a story to me about an experience he had sitting at a beach with headphones on while tripping. The waves of the sea coming to shore became synchronised with the music, and then the rest of the world around him followed in to this synchronisation, until the music itself was being conducted by the world around him. These kinds of stories are not uncommon.

So now we know how to have an adventure without ever leaving the room – but what if you and your group all do want to go out instead of just sitting around? Great! This is the most common way that things go. The music, the deep thoughts, the contemplation of the universe; that can all wait until later or at least until the first rest stop somewhere. It is time to go out and have a real adventure.

That is not to say you can not enjoy the music, the deep thoughts and the contemplation of the universe whilst you wander; but it is fair to say that you will probably be so mystified and interested by the things you see and experience that you will not have much time for the deeper kinds of thoughts. That is quite alright though – there are many hours left of the trip and once you get back to your safe haven after having wandered, you will have plenty of time to do all of that.

Wandering around on LSD could be described as somewhat like taking a stroll through an artist's interpretation of the normal everyday world. Everything is still there that you know, but it is subtly different and altered from what you are familiar with. It is all new and all interesting. Every building, every tree, every cloud in the sky will take on new aspects that you will want to appreciate.

Dealing with people can be problematic. To others that are not aware you have taken LSD, you will likely appear completely normal for the most part. You can walk straight, you can speak normally (although your speech style and topics may be drastically altered), and you can generally deal with activities like waiting for the appropriate signal when it is safe to cross the road. However to you, some of these tasks may seem daunting or difficult at the time (it gets easier after a *lot* of experience; but even for me, it is still less than preferable). Because of this, it is generally better to find an environment where little to no interaction with people outside your group is necessary. For your first time, I would call this a 'must' and allow you to make the decision for trips after that.

I have taken LSD in many different settings; but my two favourites of all time are the walkways over the headlands at Bondi Beach in Sydney, Australia; and the Eilenriede Forest in Hannover, Germany. Both of course in the evening and night when there are the fewest people around.

The first thing to decide when beginning to wander is where you will go. You do not need to plan in advance what you will do there – just be certain you have an agreed upon destination. If multiple nearby destinations are possible, plan one first with the possibility of others afterwards. As said, you have got plenty of time.

I'd advise against your destination being more than around an hour walk away – purely because it's going to take you that long to get back again. After you have spent several hours wandering, it may be a dismal prospect to consider that it is an hour back again. Once you are more experienced, you can go further if you choose – it is just a matter of being aware enough to plan the return trip whilst tripping, which is something that most people will not be able to manage on their first time.

If you are lucky enough to live in a city with beautiful architecture (as much of Europe does) and it is not too crowded, it definitely is not a bad idea to plan your wandering to take you through the city on the way to your destination. The typical European 'grand old buildings' can appear especially interesting due to the rough stonework combined with intricate detail and artisanry. Unless you are sure however that it is going to remain quiet and secluded for several hours, I strongly advise against the city being a destination in and of itself.

Assuming that it is night, the best streets to wander are those that are away from the typical nightlife. In the state of mind that

STRUCTURE OF THE TRIP

you are in, dealing with drunken people coming out of bars or clubs; or having to navigate your way around a crowd of people lined up to get in somewhere are hassles you would much rather avoid.

On the way to your destination, talk to the others that you are with. Point out things that look amazing to you and they will do the same for you. There is a good chance that you will even be able to agree on aspects of the visual effects that you see. You can stop and take as many breaks as you like along the way. Finding a place to sit and watch something particularly interesting (which may in fact be something as normally uninteresting as a house that happened to take your attention) can be one of the points that you use as a reference when sorting out the trip in your head towards the end of the trip or the next day. Just because your destination is only thirty minutes walking distance, it does not mean you can't take a couple of hours doing it if that's the way things go.

Once you reach your destination, you will need to find something to do. If you have not already stopped and sat around enough, immediately upon reaching the destination is a good time to do so. It will give you a chance to transition the setting from 'travelling there' to 'being there' in your head as well as allow you to plan the next activities. If you have not already stopped and sat around at all on the journey to the destination, I would even consider this a 'must' as you take the time to sort out your state of mind before the setting changes yet again.

The destination itself may have things for you to do. Children's playgrounds can be a source of great amusement for a period of time. I myself love swings – whether I have taken LSD or not – but especially when I have. Alternatively, as with many public forests, there may be walkways to explore or interesting statues and monuments to look at. If your trip is powerful enough of course, even looking at trees, the ground or most especially the sky can be sources of great amusement, interest and even wonder.

Once you feel you have done all you want to do at this destination, you may choose another, or you may decide to go back and enjoy the trip further in the comfort of your safe haven.

Moments of lucidity

Whether you were wandering around, still are wandering around or never went out at all, somewhere between the third and fifth hour after the trip started in full you will find – quite suddenly – that there are a few moments of complete lucidity and 'normalcy'. You are likely concerned the LSD may be wearing off early, especially if this is around the third hour.

Don't worry – it is not. This is perfectly normal as the LSD is over the peak and simultaneously your brain is beginning to slowly get used to this new order of chaos and is trying to re-establish the filters that define the 'normal world' for you.

Simply sitting back and relaxing somewhere, you will find the visuals return with quite some force, and you will lapse back in to the trip very easily.

At this stage, I actually advise 'practicing' changing your viewpoint from 'tripping' to 'normal' and back again several times. Once you have mastered this, you will find that control over your feelings from this point on – and any subsequent LSD trips in the future – are easier to manage. The best way to practice this is to concentrate on something structured, such as mathematical equations, simple processes that you are familiar with (perhaps the process of unlocking your smart-phone for example) or so on. This should take you from 'tripping' to 'normal' (at least for a short time). You can then get back to 'tripping' simply by relaxing your mind and letting it wander.

Whether it's deliberately induced or a random moment of lucidity, you'll be unlikely to hold a 'normal' state for any extended period of time, but of course, the trip is far from over, so you shouldn't consider this to be particularly surprising or problematic.

Once you are significantly more experienced, controlling these moments of lucidity becomes easier and by this stage of the trip, you truly can turn them off and on at will. As they first begin, holding a 'normal' state requires effort and towards the end, holding a 'tripping' state requires effort, but from the very first unexpected state of lucidity, it becomes possible (if somewhat unpleasant) to remain in this state. I have explained this to people who have had LSD once or twice and universally they have told me that they do not think it is possible, so I am quite confident when I say that the vast majority of people will not be able to do so at first. Like I said though – don't worry about it – let it happen, enjoy it, and revisit this if and when you have become more accustomed to the LSD state of mind.

During some lucid moments, you may contemplate the idea of going to bed and sleeping. You say to yourself that you have had a good trip, but it has been mentally (and maybe physically) exhausting, so why not just let it be over? However, you would most likely experience that you have in fact forgotten what 'tired' actually means even if 'exhausted' still makes sense. It is not that you are not tired, nor is it that you are. The very idea is meaningless to you at this stage.

Simply put, unless you truly have not slept for several days (in which case, taking LSD was a very bad idea to begin with), you will not be able to sleep and would probably just end up frustrating yourself if you tried. By all means, go to bed if you want and enjoy the patterns behind your closed eyelids combined with some beautiful mental imagery, but do not be too disappointed or upset when you are getting up again in a few minutes.

If by chance you are still wandering around at this stage, it is a strong indicator that it is time to consider heading back to your safe haven. It's by no means mandatory – if you want to continue wandering, by all means do so – but you'll likely want to return at some point not too far from now, so steering your wandering back in the direction of your safe haven is certainly highly advisable (especially if you're some quite some distance away).

Chill out

By now, you should back somewhere warm and comfortable such as your 'safe haven'. You are still tripping, but it is all becoming less intense and controlling it is now effortless even for a first timer. You can hold longer periods of lucidity if you want and might even be able to sleep if you really are tired and exhausted enough from all of your activity (although it's still quite unlikely, so again, you really should not be disappointed if you can't).

This may be a good time to begin reflecting on the trip so far. You have experienced a very great deal over the last five and a half to eight hours. Very likely, you have experienced more than any other similar time span that you can remember.

If you're feeling up to it, you may want to use this time to take a few notes about your feelings or any insights that are still fresh in your mind. If not however, don't worry – you will remember it all tomorrow and for a long time to come with near crystal clarity; the only thing that may be lost as more time passes is some of the more intricate details of how you came to the ideas and thoughts that you did.

Personally, I like to use this time for a more self-indulgent kind of enjoyment. If I am with friends (as I usually am), I may spend a little time chatting to them, but ultimately I prefer to end up lying somewhere quite still, staring at the ceiling and allow the visuals to work some magic in my mind. I do not think about anything in particular and I try to avoid the deeper, more complex thoughts that I enjoy around the peak of the trip. Simple, self-indulgent pleasure time for a while.

Music is of course also very good at this stage of the trip as with many others. Your ability to decipher the fine details as at the height of the trip are likely to be deteriorating a little and so you'll probably find that it's simply enjoyable to listen to any music that you happen to like.

The end

The trip really is wearing off now. Normalcy is returning piece by piece. The visual distortions are pretty much gone, but everything seems bright, fresh and somehow more beautiful than before. You are tired, but you can deal with it. Your chances of being able to sleep at this stage are significantly higher if you choose to, however it is definitely still just a choice: you could have been out the whole night and continue through the next day until you finally crash – completely exhausted – the following night.

It is possible that at this point, you are feeling a little 'drained' or 'done'. This does not happen to everyone, and I myself have only really started experiencing it as I have gotten older. It is not a horrible feeling, just slightly unpleasant. It's similar to the feeling you have after a long day of office work, where you've been concentrating too long and too hard and can finally let it all go for now.

If you decide not to sleep, you may use this time for some reflection on the trip; or if you're feeling drained and not up to that kind of thought, simply putting the TV on, playing some reasonably mindless video games, or other passive activities will likely tide you through the end.

Reflection

Throughout the next day, colours remain a little brighter and more vivid; and everything seems somehow good and 'right'. You are probably more tired than usual due to a lack of sleep – if you had any at all, chances are it was shorter than usual – but it was all worth it.

Whether you already reflected a little towards the end of the trip or not, now is the time that I really recommend you do so. You have a lot to process now that normalcy is back. You can remember everything that happened and that you thought about, so now is a good time to do something with it while it is still all fresh in your mind.

As you read this, before you have taken your first trip, you might wonder what I mean by 'reflection' and why you would want to do this. Indeed, especially if you have used other substances or even used psychedelics in low-dose purely for having fun, the concept might seem a little strange to you. Basically, what I mean when I say 'reflection' is to look back on the events that happened, how you felt about them, what you thought about, and how you might be able to learn something from it.

I will go in to a lot more detail on the core theme of this book – using LSD for self-discovery – in a later chapter. For now, just think of it as applying newfound knowledge of a kind that you were not previously aware of to your life in order to better it in some way.

Tales of some first trips

*"LSD burst over the dreary domain of the constipated
bourgeoisie like the angelic herald of a new psychedelic
millennium. We have never been the same since, nor
will we ever be, for LSD demonstrated, even to skeptics,
that the mansions of heaven and gardens of paradise
lie within each and all of us."*

Terence McKenna

My First Trip

My first LSD trip did not benefit from a guide. I did not know anything about LSD other than that it was a drug being offered to me, and consequently I had no idea what to expect from the trip. It was a harrowing and disturbing experience. Nevertheless, parts of it were enlightening, beautiful and stay with me to this very day.

I was nineteen years old. At the time, I was living in a shared accommodation with two other young men and one young woman. One of the men, let's call him Chris (because that was his name) was a small-time drug dealer – nothing big, but enough that he could cover his rent and other such things.

Because of Chris's occupation, we of course often had drugs around the house. I had experimented with many different things while living there; but found the experience lacking for the majority of them. Prior to living there, I had only ever tried alcohol, nicotine (in the form of cigarettes) and marijuana – pretty standard for the youth of my generation. While there, I had gone through many kinds of amphetamines, stimulants, and depressants.

One of Chris's regular customers asked if he was able to get some LSD. This was something Chris did not normally deal in, as it is not a common request and the profit margin is generally quite low if you are not a manufacturer. Nevertheless, he wanted to keep his regular customer happy and so acquired a 'sheet' of LSD blotter and sold twenty-five of the tabs to this regular. That left him with around a hundred and seventy five tabs of LSD on his hands and not a lot of customers who were so interested in it.

A few days later, we had some guests over and were all drinking pre-mixed cans of Jack Daniels and Cola. Most of us had also had a line or two of cocaine and speed. At that point, Chris pulled out the LSD and suggested we all take some.

As mentioned, I did not know what to expect, so I happily agreed, perhaps anticipating something like Ecstasy or similar, but I truly do not recall anymore as I was quite inebriated already. I was handed three tabs and put them all in my mouth at once.

I continued drinking and after around thirty minutes began to feel a little strange. The conversations around me began to become like random noise rather than real voices, and I felt a little queasy. I looked at Chris and he grinned, his grin widening beyond what a normal face is able to do.

As it was a weeknight and most of us (including myself) had work the next day, most of our guests began to leave. I suddenly realised that I had been sitting quietly for quite some time and not responding to people talking to me. I leapt up and in a panic said goodbye to the last people leaving as if it were the most important thing I had ever had to do. I just felt an urgency that one must in these situations say goodbye and by not doing so, I was somehow violating a golden rule of the universe.

I had stopped drinking, and had no more interest in the cocaine and speed that was still in plentiful supply. I told our female roommate that I would go to bed and try to get some sleep. After all, I should work tomorrow as well. She laughed and asked me if I had never taken LSD before. It was then I realised that I had never actually told anyone this was my first time.

My roommates gathered around me and explained that I was not going to be sleeping. Not for a long time. So, said Chris, I may as well just have another tab of acid. Apparently he had sold the rest to our guests and there was just one left (of this, I am still doubtful, however that was what was explained to me and I did not see the rest of the sheet after that).

I was in such a state of confusion and the ways my roommates were talking was not helping. They were tricking me, deceiving me, in to taking that tab. They just wanted to see what would happen to this poor first timer taking such a large combined dose.

Against reason, I took the tab and then lay down on the couch. I felt the alcohol and other drugs slowly wearing off, and as they did, the confusion began to fade from my mind and the stronger sensory effects of the LSD began to kick in.

I watched the patterns in the room shift in beautiful but terrifying ways. I feared I may have lost my mind, as surely the effects should be over or nearly over. I had only eaten four very small squares of cardboard after all! But no, it continued, and even continued to increase in intensity.

I have no idea what my roommates were doing at the time. I had lost all sense of them being there. The couch I was on became a bed. The bed became a waterbed. A glance at a spot of red transformed it to a waterbed full of warm blood. The roughness of the wall beside me became writhing worms. The black spots on the wall where it was not perfectly clean became the mouths of the worms coming out of the wall.

I panicked. I probably cried.

I stood up – forcing myself away from the view of the wall – and tried to make my way to the bathroom. The idea of touching the door handle for some reason scared and repulsed me. I fought with it with my elbows until it was finally open.

Using the toilet was a disgusting and horrid experience. Thinking of how my body was working and then watching this stream of filth pass out of me and into the bowl. I hurriedly washed my hands and then quickly went to my bed to lie down instead of back to the couch.

Then finally, the fear was gone. I realised what was happening; everything that was going on was purely in my own mind – manifested from my thoughts and imagination. Nothing here could harm me. Nothing here was to be feared.

I began to experiment with my mind. I watched myself thinking something and then analysed that thought process as it happened. I watched myself watching and analysed that further. I realised I was doing something that I'd never been able to do before – truly step outside of myself and watch my thoughts as an independent observer. It was fascinating.

Several hours later, I was so drained from the experience, but things were beginning to start making sense again. I looked at the clock; it was 4:30 AM.

I was due to be in to work in three and a half hours. I was still incapable of sleep. I turned on the TV and slowly normalcy returned.

I showered, changed my clothes and headed in to work. During the walk to work, I noticed how bright and clear everything seemed. The air smelled fresh and I was more alert than anyone who has not slept all night really has any right to be.

When I got to work, the screensavers on the computer monitors was set to some 3D bouncing text that was popular at that time. It seemed to be almost coming out of the monitors at me and I had to look away.

By halfway through my twelve hour shift I was totally exhausted. The lack of sleep had caught up with me and combined with the extreme mental workout that I had not been prepared for, was almost too much for me to handle. I finally finished my shift, headed home, and slept right through to the next morning.

This experience may sound more negative than positive; and you may be surprised that I ever took LSD again after this. But the panic and the fear that seemed to last forever at the time were more than offset by the positive aspects. And I somehow knew that if I took it again, I would be able to control myself better. I would understand that I had nothing to fear and make better use of the experience to examine my perception of myself and the world around me in even more detail.

I never again experienced that terror or fear. Even after hundreds of trips, because I now know what I learned that first time – it is all in my mind. I can use it, shape it, control it, and learn from it. I need not fear it.

If someone had told me beforehand what you are now reading in this book, I am sure I would have never had a 'bad trip' ever; but in some ways I'm glad I did, because this realisation has stayed with me throughout my life and helped shape so many other decisions.

Janet's Experience

Janet is a friend of a friend. She hails from Australia and came to Germany to visit our mutual friend, Sebastian.

Janet had not had a real LSD trip before, and after hearing about it was interested in trying it. At that point, this book that you are now reading was a short six page 'how to' leaflet and I provided it to her as a kind of preparation for the experience.

As the weather was not good and we wanted to have somewhere we could retire back to in warmth and comfort without disturbing others, we rented a hotel room near the heart of the city.

Janet, Sebastian and I met together at the train station near the hotel and headed there in the early evening. We talked briefly about the upcoming experience and then took the LSD. Janet and Sebastian both took two and a half tabs of a fairly weak blotter that I had – around 125µg to 150µg in total – well within the range that I would recommend in general. I myself had three and a half tabs of the same LSD – so, somewhere between175µg and 210µg – quite a moderate trip for me; but I wanted to remain capable of serving as a guide for the trip if need be.

Everything started very well. We talked for a bit and waited for the trip to start. Janet was anxious for it to come on soon, and perhaps at first felt like nothing (or even just very little) was going to happen.

I began to experience the first feelings of the trip and then shortly afterwards some minor visual effects on a table that were only there when I really looked for them. I mentioned this to the others but Janet was still 'not sure' if anything was happening.

My trip began to take a stronger hold and Janet had fallen silent. Sebastian and I continued to chat and watching Janet, I assumed she was still in the early stages of the trip, wondering if it was really there or not. She slowly began to join in the conversation, and it was clear that she was indeed tripping to an extent. Later she told me that despite her general silence, this was a truly wonderful part of the trip for her. I suggested we head out for a walk if everyone felt up to it. There were no objections raised, so out we went.

At first, Janet made some comments about the pretty buildings around but it was clear her trip was starting to take a stronger hold and she seemed a little uneasy. Sebastian and I became her 'protectors' ensuring her safety from the big world that she found herself in.

Our walk took us down a street that first led past a crowd of people trying to enter a nightclub – something that none of us were happy being around. It then led to some rather dull suburbia and none of us were particularly happy with that either. It was suggested we should perhaps head to the forest, getting out of the city lights; and so we headed then in that direction. Janet had fallen quite silent for a while and attempts to engage her were met with little response. I felt perhaps she was becoming a little terrified by the chaos of the city around us and so wholeheartedly agreed with the forest as a location. On the way, there were some police doing something and Janet seemed uncomfortable with their presence. We just assured her that it would all be okay and kept walking – there were, of course, no problems.

We did not make it as far as the forest. On the way, Janet stopped us and said that she just could not do it anymore. It had to end now. This is always a terrible thing to get in to your head, because there's no way it possibly can end – that early in the trip it is going to keep on continuing for many hours to come; and those hours themselves will feel like an eternity.

From what Janet was saying, we realised she was having a problem with scale as will be described later in the chapter "Don't Panic". The outside world was simply too large for her, too big, and too much. She simply was not prepared to take in that much and it scared her.

We decided the best course of action was to forget the forest and get back to the hotel room. Somewhere smaller where she did not have to deal with such a 'big' universe around her. As we headed back, my suspicions were confirmed as she kept repeating the request to, 'make it all smaller', and 'make it stop'. Sebastian and I helped her by talking and giving her mental imagery of her being a mouse, safe and secure in its little mouse hole. Janet later told me that this had helped her significantly.

The walk back to the hotel room was difficult. Janet's sense of time and distance were becoming quite distorted and the last hundred metres or so to the hotel took us much longer than anticipated as she felt we had been walking for a very long time and that we somehow would have to walk for even longer still to arrive back at the hotel. Eventually though, of course we did. We closed the door and let Janet lie down on the bed. Sebastian put some music on.

This helped Janet's state of mind greatly, but it still was not easy for her. At first, she asked if it would be over soon, and if she could sleep. Of course she could try, but we knew full well that it would not be possible. There were still many hours left.

Now that the input of the world around her had shrunk down to a manageable level, her mind began to work on creating its own universe. In some ways, I consider myself a little to blame at this point, as the concept of universe-building was already in the small leaflet that I had written and she was clearly latching on to this as something that her mind 'should be doing'.

Janet's new universe is not something I can tell you much about, as she spoke only in snippets of what was clearly a much more complex process in her mind. What seems clear is that it was a replacement universe for the real one. Events from this one 'had happened' in hers, if she declared them to be the case. Time in her universe however seemed to be problematic for her – events were numbered and attempted to be sequenced. These were both real events, and 'building' events. Things such as "have I invented breathing[1] yet?" followed by "yes, but that was after I lay down" and "those are numbers thirty five and twenty six". For a while, she also seemed to have lost her ability to handle language and was making sounds that did not correspond to words that I could recognise at all.

In a later conversation, Janet told me that in normal day to day life, she tries to be very ordered and organised. Categorising things and having a detailed calendar helps her to take control of her life. The numbering of items for her was an attempt to do this to order the trip. It however was too much for her to

---

[1] At no point did Janet stop breathing, nor was there any risk of this. No matter how deep in the trip you are, your body's automatic reflexes will win out still and even if you were to deliberately stop breathing for whatever reason, you'll start again very soon just as you would when not taking LSD.

manage with her ego as lost as it was and she described it as being "*what happens when I'm not there to be in charge of myself for imposing that control.*"

Slowly but surely, Janet's trip began to wear off and with it, the returning sureness allowed her to truly start enjoying the trip again. She became more coherent and talkative and started to talk about how beautiful everything was. We had had a recurring theme in our earlier conversations of things being "*mit Sparkles*" ('mit' is German for 'with' and she enjoyed using this word) and she described this enjoyable latter part of the trip as being "*very much mit Sparkles*".

The sun rose and normalcy returned as it always does; with three exhausted, but happy mental explorers. We checked out of the hotel and returned to the train station where we parted ways.

Janet at first was embarrassed to talk to me about the trip – concerned that her inability to handle a large part of it was somehow something to be ashamed of. I assured her it was okay and then she opened up to me that it was on the whole a wonderful and positive experience despite the negative part. It was more '*terrific*' than '*terrible*' and she is keen to try it again with me one day (most likely in Australia where her surroundings are more familiar and comfortable). She even thanked me for the experience.

Whilst writing this book, I discussed this trip further with Janet to try to get more of an understanding of what was happening from her perspective rather than just my own. She told me that one of her main difficulties during the trip came from the way that time was no longer so linear. What had happened before the trip and what happened during had become muddled to her, as with a dream that is all too real. She had tried to sort it out in her mind, but had become frustrated by her inability to do so, and so missed much of the enjoyment as she fought with these thoughts.

For a time, apparently, she thought that perhaps she had died. This did not bother her so much, but she was concerned about her mother. She was aware that in reality she was alive, but kept fighting the urge to break away completely and disappear in to her own mind. She wanted to keep a hold on some kind of reality and used the sense of touch with physical objects to ground herself to the real world.

From my perspective, this was perhaps a mistake on her part. While being grounded to reality is generally a good thing in many circumstances; at that point, we were safe and secure in our hotel room and had she just let reality go for a while, many of the concerns and worries that were making it difficult for her may have dissolved along with it. Reality does come back eventually, and so assuming the environment allows it, letting it disappear for a while is certainly not a bad thing to do.

Janet did however also tell me that I must say how much she enjoyed the beginning of the trip, as we sat and talked about random things. She was apparently tripping more than I realised at that point and had experienced true delight. Reminders of it for her bring back feelings of genuine joy.

In summary, a large part of Janet's trip was less positive than it could have been. Some of it was even quite horrible. But overall, she considers it a positive experience nonetheless. The negative parts of her trip were, in a way, one of the influences on me that helped me make the decision to expand my small leaflet in to this book that you are reading now.

A More Positive Trip

After reading about my first trip and Janet's trip; despite my reassurances, you may fear that all first trips contain a negative experience. This is far from the case. So, as a counterpoint, I would like now to tell you about a much more typical trip that I had after I had become much more familiar with LSD.

The trip was taken with two very close friends of mine – Sebastian and Peter – around eight or nine years ago. It was the first trip for Sebastian and one of the early times (but not the first) for Peter. For myself, it was towards the start of the phase where I was starting to realise the strong influence of LSD on my life rather than only 'just having fun' with the experience. We were all living in Sydney, Australia at the time and Sebastian's small apartment served as a common location for us to meet up before going out or doing things.

We all met up at Sebastian's apartment as usual and decided that an appropriate location for the trip would be the headlands around Bondi Beach. This is still one of my favourite places to this day, but I had not been there before while tripping. We took the LSD – if I recall correctly, around 200µg for myself and somewhere around 100µg for the others – sometime in the mid to late afternoon and then began the journey to the beach. To get there, we needed to first make our way to the centre of Bondi followed by a short bus ride.

I do not recall how we made it to Bondi, but I know that the trip had not really started to come on very strongly until we were there. As we waited for the bus, I began to feel that everything was far more humorous than it really ought to be. I was laughing at almost everything and when Sebastian said something funny to me (lost in the mists of time now I am afraid) I laughed so hard that I felt I might not be able to come up for air again.

Eventually the bus arrived and we got on. The patterned seats of the Sydney Buses provided an interesting – if somewhat shocking – introduction to the first strong visuals of the trip. To me, the seats were writhing as if almost alive, and I felt as if the people sitting in them were somehow being disrespectful of the seats by the callous nature in which they ignored them and simply treated them as furniture. At no point do I recall thinking about the seat that I was sitting in however. Sebastian told me later that he also experienced very strong visuals from the seats; and beyond that, his recollection of the bus ride also includes a woman that appeared to strongly disapprove of our being there. If I ever saw her myself, I do not recall.

Once we reached the beach, I felt quite relieved to get off the bus. Being trapped, somewhat immobile, in a moving vehicle with a large number of complete strangers that are not under the influence of LSD is not the best of experiences in general. It was not however too uncomfortable as I was prepared for this to be the case and was able to put it out of my mind quickly after getting off the bus.

Once at the beach, the first thing we did was to stand at one of the raised platforms overlooking the sand. It was early evening at that stage, but with plenty of light still remaining. The patterns of the sand stay with me to this day as one of the most beautiful visual effects I have ever experienced on LSD. The complex patterns naturally in the sand, caused by wind, people and whatever else, moved in impossible ways and the sea air only helped to invigorate me – thus the visuals also – whipping the effect in to an orchestral frenzy for the eyes. Sebastian did not seem too interested in the sand at this stage and Peter specifically commented that he did not see much in the way of visuals at all.

After this, we spent a short while sitting on the grass behind the beach and waiting for the number of people around to decrease as it got darker. This happened fairly quickly – or at least, I do not recall a significant amount of time sitting there.

As it started becoming darker and the people at the beach began to leave, we made our way to the headlands; briefly pausing by the same spot as before to look at the sand. This time, both Sebastian and Peter commented on how amazing it seemed to them also.

Following the walkway around for a little, you soon find yourself at some old stone stairs, partially hewn from the rock itself and partially built according to the need. Standing at the bottom of the stairs looking up at them, we were all immediately shocked and impressed to find that the angles and grade involved with them seemed completely impossible. We quickly dubbed them the "stairs of insanity" and spent a little time debating whether or not it was really possible to climb them. Logic and reason of course won out in the end as we decided that it was of course only the LSD changing our perception in this way and the stairs were probably quite reasonable despite their appearance to us.

We climbed the stairs easily and without incident, however as I reached the top and turned around to look behind me, I was struck again by the impossible angles and this time also the height of the stairs. I felt a moment of doubt that I had truly just climbed them.

At the top of the stairs, I had failed to notice at first that there was in fact a second, somewhat shorter but still seemingly impossible, set of stairs heading further up. Before braving those stairs, we decided to pause and take note of the universe around us.

Peter began to tell us a story about the thoughts that were going on in his mind. As he did, he used a lot of hand and body gestures to demonstrate his point. I sat and watched him pacing and waving his arms and felt true camaraderie with these two explorers that were with me. Peter then got to a crescendo in his story and raised both arms simultaneously up and to the sides. To my eyes, the clouds behind him shifted away from the movement; Peter was an all-powerful being – a demi-god – and even the clouds in the sky respected and feared him. Interestingly, Peter later related to me that my description of this to him was enough for him to also be able to see this happening from my perspective.

We walked further around the headlands and talked about anything and everything that came to our minds. At a couple of stages, I felt a little concerned about how close to the edge of the sudden drop down to the ocean that Sebastian and Peter were getting at times, however in reality, there was plenty of space and none of us were in any danger of falling.

After a while, we decided we had walked far enough and turned around to head back. As we turned, I suddenly felt the whole world change with my change of direction. The colour of the sky was different; the sound of the sea was different; and the way the air felt on my skin was different. It wasn't better, nor was it worse – only different.

We had spent the entire time smoking many cigarettes, as smokers will almost always do when tripping. However it wasn't until we were heading back that Sebastian suddenly exclaimed his lighter wasn't producing a flame, but rather "emitting pixels" that would light his cigarette as if they were little sparks. I thought this sounded like a wonderful visual effect and lamented that my lighter appeared to be doing no such thing – in fact, my lighter was not working very well at all. I borrowed Sebastian's lighter to light my cigarette and to my amazement and wonder, I experienced the same effect that Sebastian did – his lighter did indeed emit pixels, as if from an RGB television or computer monitor – and they flew from the lighter to my cigarette, setting it alight.

The final part of the walk back to the beach involved walking along beside the bottom of one of the cliff faces of the headlands. As we walked, we all had the same distinct impression of looking at ourselves from out on the ocean, walking along through an oil painting – to Sebastian, specifically along the lines of Vincent van Gogh's "Starry Night" – with no dimensionality to it at all. This was very beautiful to me and I wished (and still wish) that I had artistic talent to try to recreate that image on a canvas.

We arrived back at the beach, which is backed by a row of shops. Someone needed to purchase something – perhaps cigarettes, but I truly do not recall anymore. Sebastian decided he was able to deal with people well enough to walk in to the shop and make the purchase. After he came out, he told us the story of how the shop had appeared to him. As he stepped in to the shop, it was flat and two dimensional, but instead of being a static image or an oil painting like the landscape, it was instead more like a flip book. Each step forward it would flip to the new scene. Walking faster made it flip faster, and walking slower made it flip slower. It also worked in reverse, where walking backwards – as he did to leave the shop – caused it to flip to the new scene as well. As soon as he left the shop, the illusion was gone.

The boulevard in front of Bondi Beach is relatively busy, even in to the early hours of the morning. As we walked further along, Sebastian experienced a new illusion whereby people's ages were shifting. He would see a young girl that would become an old woman as we approached, or an old woman that would transform to youthful beauty as we went past. As he explained it to me, I was able to see it as well; however the effect did not last as long for me as it seemed to for him.

To get away from the crowds, we returned to the beach itself and lay, looking up at the sky – remaining silent for long periods, but talking occasionally about the things we saw, felt and experienced. Sebastian was deep in an illusion, both visually and mentally. He saw the face of an Indian goddess formed from the sky itself watching him from above. At first, it really worried him as – being his first trip – he had never really experienced anything like that at all, but that feeling went away quite quickly and he felt reassured as he saw that the goddess was smiling at him. Later, he remarked that one thing he found odd is that it was an Indian goddess, as he was raised in a Christian household.

Before returning home to Sebastian's apartment, we decided to get something to drink at the Bondi Hotel – a pub on a corner near the beach. The light-shades inside were strange bulbous things and were swelling and retracting for us. Attempting to head to the bar to purchase the drinks, I felt very out of place and uncomfortable with the bar-flies inhabiting the pub at that hour and quickly went back to our seats outside instead. I believe Peter then purchased the drinks for us and Sebastian went to the toilet.

Peter wanted to 'damp down' the end of the trip and decided to drink a beer. I was enjoying the experience too much – and as mentioned, prefer not to do that during a trip – and so had a tall glass of sparkling lemonade. The lemonade was one of the most interesting experiences with the sensation of touch that I have ever had, and unfortunately, while I still greatly enjoy a glass of lemonade while on LSD (far more than when not); I have never yet had a repeat of that feeling to the same degree. What was so special was the way that the carbon dioxide bubbles formed in the liquid. I could hold the lemonade in my mouth and feel the unique shape of each bubble as it formed on my tongue, broke free and then disintegrated on the roof of my mouth. Each individual bubble. I am absolutely certain that I will remember this sensation for the rest of my life.

Sebastian returned from the toilet looking quite disturbed. He related to us that he had had difficulty deciding on which urinal to use. At that point, a man walked in and asked, "*Tough choice?*" to which Sebastian had apparently simply replied, "*You have no idea*".

As we sat and talked, I was somewhat disgusted by the smell of Peter's beer and the very concept that he could be drinking it. However then I was distracted by Sebastian. He appeared to me to be almost 'elven' in appearance – somewhere between a pixie and an angel. His skin seemed smooth and taut across his thin face, but not gaunt. His smile seemed wise and knowing; and his countenance suggested grace and elegance without even moving and yet there was also a hint of mischief in the corner of the smile[1].

In order to return to Sebastian's apartment, the best choice seemed to be a taxi. I can not tell you what time of night it was – only that it was quite likely sometime in the early hours of the morning. Our journey around the headlands had taken a significant amount of time. The taxi driver was thankfully quiet and did not try to talk to us on the journey – I at least certainly would not have been able to deal with that level of conversation particularly easily. The journey seemed to take a lifetime, with the streets that I should have known so well all appearing alien and strange right up until we had reached the apartment again. Finally, we were there and I escaped out of the taxi in to the night air, feeling as if I had just endured a horror and triumphantly come out of it unscathed.

Back in Sebastian's apartment, we first attempted to play PacMan™ for no sensible reason that I can recall. While PacMan is in some ways one of my specialities normally, I was completely unable to manage it in that state. We then switched to watching the movie *"A Scanner Darkly"* – very probably a bad idea in general for reasons that I have stated in previous chapters, but for the most part, I simply ignored it and let my mind wander.

---

[1] It is worth mentioning again that as someone with Asperger's syndrome, it is generally impossible for me to be able to perceive things such as people's faces in this abstract way. Not only was the LSD providing the altered perception of Sebastian's appearance, but for me, also the ability to even make this kind of perception.

Finally, after the movie was over, I lay on the floor, with only a rolled up coat as a pillow below my head. We talked for a while more and simply enjoyed the tail end of the trip. Sebastian reported an interesting visual effect from looking at/out the window, as it seemed the world outside was rocking, as if the apartment were a boat and he was looking out as the boat rocked on the sea.

At a point later in the discussion, the conversation included a lot of the phrase *"ultimately I would like to"*, talking about the future. I was mostly however just distracted my own thoughts still and chimed in once with, *"Ultimately I would like to get a haircut tomorrow"* in an attempt to lighten the conversation a little and also hopefully end it. After a while, we fell silent and I spent what felt like an eternity or two simply continuing to stare at the ceiling as I had been throughout our conversation. The visual effects were still quite strong and I watched as green lightning flickered through the patterns in the ceiling – forming geometric shapes of increasing complexity until I blinked and then starting again from the basics.

At some point, I fell asleep, but as is often the case with LSD trips, the line between awake and asleep can be difficult to judge. I only know that after a while I was waking up – implying I must have slept – to sunlight streaming in the window, bright beautiful colours on everything, and a feeling of great contentment and well-being.

Dangers and risks

"After all, even the most positive LSD experiences often involve disturbing visions and moments of paranoia. Most of us still managed to do OK during our first time, maybe even were steered toward an epiphany. But some of us didn't. Some of us crash-landed and injured ourselves or others, or were overpowered by unresolved subconscious conflicts."

Tim Doody, "The Heretic", The Morning News

So, what **are** the possible dangers of LSD?

The first and perhaps most important danger is a lower acceptance of the meaning of your surroundings. Dangerous situations should be avoided carefully whilst tripping. While you will most likely be consciously aware of danger, the idea may seem a little more abstract than usual – as with almost all ideas – and so you may be less careful than otherwise.

A tale was related to me where a person in a group that had all taken LSD was playing a guitar with a piece of broken glass. He accidentally cut himself with the glass, and the remainder of the group simply found it amazing and somewhat funny at how red the blood was instead of paying attention to the mortal danger that he was in.

Dehydration from wandering around for extended periods is another potential concern. LSD itself does not generally dehydrate you, however as you are more active, possibly sweating more, and are likely to spend quite some time walking around; it is possible that if you do not pay attention to your liquid intake, you will find yourself becoming dehydrated. I have personally never encountered a situation where this is a problem, however it has been reported to me by several people as being a possible concern and the reasoning makes sense.

Misjudging the actions or intentions of others can also in some cases lead to problems. You will likely not want to interact with people that are not tripping with you; but if you do, you need to pay closer attention to their behaviour than you normally would, as you may miss or misinterpret clues about their behaviour. Having some angry skinhead beat you up because you thought he was a friendly looking man and tried to start a conversation would not be a good thing. Overall this falls in to the same category as 'dangerous situations' in general though, as simply putting yourself in the kind of environment where this kind of thing could happen would have been a failure on your part to choose an appropriate setting for the trip.

During pregnancy, LSD may in theory cause miscarriage. There is no specific documented evidence of this danger, however as other close chemical relations to LSD are designed to assist bringing on labour through uterine contractions, the risk is simply not worth it. Even if you do not miscarry, should the baby's brain be developed enough, it may be born with a kind of post-traumatic stress disorder (the baby **almost definitely** will experience a trip; which without an adult mind to process it, could in theory be an extremely traumatic experience). Relatedly of course, breastfeeding mothers should avoid any drugs that may be passed through in breast milk – including LSD. Quite simply, if you are a pregnant or breastfeeding woman it is highly irresponsible to take LSD or any other drugs not prescribed specifically by your doctor and I could never in good conscience condone doing so.

Due to the altered sense of chronoception as described earlier, misjudging time can in some cases lead to problems. You are fully aware that spending three hours sitting around in the cold at night in winter is not good for you just as you would be without being on LSD. However, if you are not aware that three hours have passed, you may find yourself negatively affected by the cold – reduced immune response to viruses and bacteria (catching a cold), or in extreme cases, frostbite. These are not likely since you are still in control of yourself and will almost certainly take action to remedy the situation if you find yourself uncomfortably cold; however, it is worth remembering that you may not be as able to accurately judge time as you normally are.

In case you have fears regarding toxicity, there are no definite figures for lethal dosages; however, experimentation with animals in the nineteen-sixties produced results showing a minimum human lethal dosage of 200µg per kilogram of body weight, up to a maximum of 1500µg per kilogram of body weight. This would mean that an eighty kilogram human would need to consume a **minimum** of **one hundred and sixty** 'good' tabs of LSD in order to have a possibly fatal effect.

There is also plenty of evidence to assume that these figures are in fact even greatly *underestimated*, as there is a known case of people that mistook LSD in crystal form for cocaine, and insufflated ('snorted') an entire gram – somewhere between five thousand and twenty thousand times a 'normal' dose. They required intensive care and possibly had internal bleeding; however, they survived and were not any worse for wear after recovering in hospital for a few days. They were comatose the entire time and did not experience any kind of a trip. As mentioned above, the most I ever consumed at once was the equivalent of only **six** such 'good' tabs – rather a significant difference.

As already mentioned, you should avoid taking LSD in combination with any other substances. I would like to expand on this, as it is an important point.

For some people, drugs are a common part of their lives. For others however, drugs are scary, forbidden, evil things that they do not even want to understand (this incidentally is what leads to a lot of very stupid legislation). For the rest of us, we are somewhere in between.

Chances are, you have had alcohol before and are familiar with the effects of having a little too much. Combining alcohol with another substance will generally put the effects of both substances on top of each other. That is, you could be both drunk and on a cocaine high at the same time. This is true of almost all drugs that alter state of mind. For the kind of person that takes a variety of drugs regularly, it's not unheard of for example to have a combination of MDMA, ketamine, GHB and cocaine all in one night, with the effects of each essentially layering on top of each other – often as one begins wearing off, another is used to take its place. Note that if this is not done with some experience, it can be extremely dangerous, but for the type of people that do this, the necessary care is generally second nature[1].

LSD and other psychedelics however are quite different. This is because LSD does not affect you like the drugs above – it instead changes your complete perception of the world.

For example, instead of having 'two different kinds of high', combining LSD with marijuana would generally lead to you being unable to handle or truly enjoy the LSD experience, as you're dulled by the marijuana's 'stone' effect; or the possible paranoia from the marijuana may trigger extreme anxiety issues as the LSD weakens your ability to reason some things out.

To be fair and avoid negative emails from regular marijuana users that have also tried LSD, it is possible for marijuana to enhance the experience of the trip significantly. This only happens though if the person is a regular marijuana user and has

---

[1] It most certainly will still have harmful effects on the body; but nowhere near as serious as you might imagine if you're the kind of person who is shocked by hearing about this kind of behaviour.

'exactly the right amount' of marijuana. Too little will have no influence on the trip and too much will cause the trip to become unmanageable. For this reason, I would never recommend this unless you are willing to experiment and possibly experience several extremely difficult trips prior to finding the balance that is right for you.

Combining LSD with alcohol tends to reduce the major effects of the LSD until the primary effects of the alcohol wear off – at which point you are likely to be both hung over and tripping at the same time, which I can (unfortunately) tell you from experience is a truly horrid feeling.

As a third example, combining LSD with something like cocaine may lead to an almost psychotic episode as you find yourself wanting to 'stand up against' this new universe that you're beginning to experience.

These examples are however purely 'state of mind' problems. If you do happen to combine LSD with other recreational substances, there are no known negative interactions that will cause serious harm (however, as explained soon, some non-recreational medications can have serious interactions). State of mind problems however should not be underestimated.

One class of drugs that does not directly have a negative interaction with LSD is MDMA (Ecstasy) and derivatives. This combination is quite common in the dance/nightclub scene and is referred to as 'candy flipping'. When candy flipping however, the MDMA almost completely takes over and there is very little effect from the LSD itself beyond some visual effects and very minor alteration of the state of mind. As the MDMA wears off, you may feel the LSD trip taking more of a hold – LSD lasts longer than MDMA – but the most interesting part of the trip is already over. In this case, the LSD is acting as little more than an additional stimulant and providing some visual effects.

MDMA itself is an interesting substance and can be used in similar ways to LSD for improving your knowledge of yourself, however the experience itself is quite different and so I will not focus on it in this book. I would still advise against this combination in general.

My good friend Sebastian likes to take a small amount of MDMA towards the end of a trip to 'smooth it off' and remove some of the anxiety. In the chapter "Structure of a Trip" earlier in this book, you may remember a description near the end of the trip where I describe feeling 'drained' or 'done'. This is the point at which Sebastian likes to use a small amount of MDMA. This itself is different to 'candy flipping' as the MDMA is taken at the tail end of the trip rather than at the start.

Another friend of mine – Peter – likes to have a small amount of alcohol around the same point at the end of a trip, effectively numbing the mind a little and cancelling out the LSD effects. As he describes it, *"you drink and end up sober"*. While this is certainly a fairly effective method for avoiding any negative feelings at the end of the trip, it again is something I would generally advise against. Instead of having the opportunity to think deeply over the trip you have just experienced, you find yourself in a lazy, relaxed state and if you have just been out all night, after a short while will have no interest in anything beyond sleep.

With regard to non-recreational drugs, LSD has very few known interactions with any other substances. If you are taking SSRI[1] antidepressants, MAOIs[2], or possibly other substances with a similar working, it may reduce the LSD effect to a degree, but it also may not. You should definitely not consider SSRIs or MAOIs as a 'quick and easy end of the trip' by any stretch of the imagination.

LSD may also have a strong negative interaction with lithium and tricyclic antidepressants. If you are taking lithium or tricyclic antidepressants, be aware that according to the current state of knowledge, **it may be very risky to take LSD**, with possible side-effects including coma or a dissociative fugue state, where you may begin to wander around on 'auto-pilot' with no control over your actions. The coma or fugue state can last significantly longer than a trip normally would – days, or even weeks.

 Other drugs such as aspirin, paracetamol (Tylenol), sleep aids, pain medication, hayfever medication (antihistamines) and so on, are not known to have any interaction with LSD one way or another.

Overall, the majority of these dangers are easy to avoid and do not require more than a moment of thought once you are familiar with the experience and have a rough idea of what to expect. For your first trip however, I do advise being aware of these and accordingly planning ahead beforehand.

---

[1] Selective Serotonin Reuptake Inhibitors

[2] Monoamine Oxidase Inhibitors

There are many stories out there about people having taken LSD and 'gone mad' in some way, causing serious injury or even death to themselves and others. The stories range from people leaping out of windows or off cliffs trying to fly; to a babysitter on LSD putting the baby in to the oven thinking it was a turkey. These stories along with the vast majority that you might come across are pure fabrication with not a shred of truth anywhere in them.

After LSD was declared an illegal drug in most of the world, many countries – and the United States especially – began a strong media campaign against LSD. There are full 'documentaries' from this era that describe only strongly negative short term effects and then even worse long term effects such as depression and psychosis with flashbacks being so strong and frequent that absolutely anyone who uses LSD will be unable to function in normal society for the rest of their life.

This is quite clearly all complete and utter rubbish; but it is the source of the vast majority of the myths that you may have heard or are likely to come across. If such effects or behaviours were known, you would expect to find evidence of actual cases in news reports or medical literature. No such evidence can be found, no matter how hard you search.

During the duration of the trip itself, it is a different matter. If you are unprepared for some elements of the experience, it is possible to find yourself entering a state of panic which – if not properly controlled – can cause you to spiral further in to such a wild state of panic that becomes increasingly difficult to get out of – the so-called 'bad trip'. What is important to realise however is that this is all in your own mind and you can prepare for it, avoid it, and get out of it if it starts happening.

A 'bad trip' has nothing to do with the 'quality' of the LSD itself. There is no such thing as 'good acid' and 'bad acid' – it either is LSD or it is not and the only difference between two different tabs in general is the quantity of LSD itself. Even on the off chance that it in fact isn't LSD at all and you're taking some other psychedelic substance with similar effects (as a first timer for example, you could hardly be expected to know the difference), there's no known chemical action that will produce a 'good' experience versus a 'bad' one – it's quite simply all in your head.

This is an important topic and as such deserves more than a side note in this chapter alone. For that reason, the next chapter "Don't Panic" covers this one topic in more depth.

It is worth qualifying the above statement that "it is or it isn't LSD" with some additional information, lest I receive a thousand letters and emails from chemists. Some LSD precursors may be found along with the pure LSD on blotter paper (or other distribution forms) as well as some chemicals that LSD decays in to. Some of these chemicals may in theory have a slightly noticeable effect – although realistically, the chance is very slim – and so 'less pure' LSD may produce somewhat noticeably different effects to LSD that is of a higher purity. However, on the balance of things, the effects of these precursors and decay chemicals is at absolute most significantly less than the effects of what you had for dinner that evening and so can generally be discounted with only a few exceptions. I will talk more about this later in the chapter titled "The Chemistry".

The myth of 'bad acid' was popularised further by an announcement made at the Woodstock festival in 1969, where an announcement was made to "stay away from the brown acid". While it is likely that some people had taken this LSD on brown blotter paper and experienced negative effects, there was almost certainly nothing special about this blotter compared to any other.

Another important effect to note is suggestibility. In a later chapter, you will read about (now public, but secret at the time) experiments were done on whether LSD may make a suitable truth serum for captured spies or other players in the world of espionage. It is not particularly suitable for this (especially not compared to the likes of Sodium Pentothal™ or other barbiturates); however the reason that it was investigated for this is the definitely valid effect of suggestibility.

A story was related to me of a woman that took LSD for the first time in a group of others. She did not know what to expect, but had heard all of the propaganda, as it was hard to ignore in the place and time she was. When the trip began in earnest, she searched in her mind for "*what does one do on LSD?*" and as she was near a window (closed) the first thought that came to her mind was, "*people on LSD jump out of windows!*" She did not jump, but simply that this thought came in to her mind shows that she had been influenced by the propaganda.

In the last chapter, you read some stories of real LSD experiences. In the story of Janet's first experience, I described how she tried to build a universe in her mind – and unfortunately failed. This action was almost certainly a direct consequence of me, well before the trip itself, having said that I enjoy doing that on a trip. I am a software developer – a creator; an architect; a builder of virtual worlds in a way. It is only natural that my mind wants to do this, as it is a strong part of what defines me as a person. Janet is not such a person. She did it because she had interpreted from my statements that "*that's what one does on LSD*".

Fortunately, simply knowing that this kind of suggestibility exists is enough to dampen it sufficiently or even nullify it in the vast majority of cases. You may find yourself thinking, "*What does one do on LSD?*" but the only answer you need to remember when this question arises in your mind is, "*what feels right*". You do not need to do what others have done, nor do you need to follow any particular thought pattern. Your thoughts and thought processes are uniquely yours. There may be some similarity with others – that's usually what leads to good friendships – but you're not the exactly same as anyone else and so there's no reason to think you should be the same as anyone else when having a psychedelic experience either.

Possible – but extraordinarily unlikely – long term negative effects of LSD are 'Hallucinogen Persisting Perception Disorder' (HPPD), flashbacks and psychosis. It is almost tempting to label them as 'myths' as with the others above, however there is a small amount of evidence – in particular edge cases only – for each of them. What definitely is a myth is that these long term effects are common and somehow a potential danger that all LSD users must be concerned about.

HPPD is a medically recognised condition and consists of 'LSD-like' disturbances of vision and other senses for extended periods of time. HPPD is almost always only sensory disturbance and does not include a change in state of mind; however, in some rare cases it has been reported. Much shorter, milder periods of sensory disturbance and feeling however are what most people refer to as 'flashbacks' and are not medically recognised as a condition.

There is at present no direct evidence that LSD causes flashbacks; however, indirect evidence exists and is still a matter of disagreement between researchers. There is absolutely no evidence that LSD causes HPPD.

If LSD does cause flashbacks, which it may do – despite that I have never experienced it myself, nor know anyone else that has – the reported prevalence of flashbacks is significantly higher than the actual number. If you have never taken a psychedelic substance and experience a moment of 'feeling a bit strange' or even have visual disturbances for a few seconds, you will likely pass it off as stress, tiredness, or other such causes. If you have taken a psychedelic substance at some point in your life however, the feeling or visual disturbances may remind you of the psychedelic experience and you then attribute it to be a flashback.

A personal experience of mine for example was after a very long drive. I was driving on relatively unfamiliar roads for over ten hours without a break. When I reached my destination, I needed to use the bathroom. I sat down in the bathroom and suddenly the tiles of the floor and walls began to move before my eyes and I felt quite 'trippy'. The feeling and the visual disturbance lasted perhaps around ten to twenty seconds at the absolute most and then was gone. It would be very easy for me to call this a 'flashback', but in reality it was far more likely that being over-tired and having kept myself awake through the concentration required for driving, my central nervous system was simply in a somewhat 'overloaded' state.

Flashbacks and HPPD are also both well-known from outside the world of psychedelics itself. They are symptoms that are associated with Post Traumatic Stress Disorder (PTSD) for example. While there does not appear to be any evidence that LSD or other psychedelics can cause PTSD, it most certainly can be an extremely traumatising experience when the environment or state of mind are not correctly managed. It is therefore not out of the realm of possibility that flashbacks are in fact a symptom of the stress and mental trauma that was experienced during the trip and not as a primary symptom of the drug itself.

It is possible that in people with pre-existing mental conditions who were likely to suffer psychotic episodes anyway, that LSD acts as a trigger to set off the episode. There is no conclusive evidence of any kind that LSD causes psychotic episodes in otherwise healthy minds. This is of course extremely difficult to judge, as it can only be stated that after having consumed LSD, an extremely small but non-zero number of people have had psychotic episodes. Perhaps these people would have anyway, but perhaps not. The only recorded evidence of such was one person out of a group of 1250. This person was an identical twin of a schizophrenic and so may well have had similar undiagnosed issues. Out of people with pre-existing mental conditions, the recorded rate of LSD inducing a psychosis is around one fifth of one percent.

Having first-hand experience of a very large number of LSD trips taken by both myself and other people, I have not seen any indication of flashbacks, HPPD, or psychotic behaviour lasting longer than the LSD trip itself.

A common fear with any drug is the fear that you will become addicted. There is nothing worse than imagining yourself on a downward spiral of drug abuse, continuing to use the substance 'just to get through the day'. This is a valid fear with many drugs, but not all. Not all drugs are addictive – some are, some are not. LSD is a completely non-addictive substance.

Understanding what addiction is and how it works goes a long way towards relieving concerns about this. Essentially, there are two kinds of addiction – 'psychological addiction' and 'physical addiction'. Almost everyone has experienced the first kind, and many people have experienced the second.

Psychological addiction is when you enjoy something so much that you want to do it again. People who are 'chocoholics' are psychologically addicted to chocolate. The only physically addictive compound we know of in chocolate is caffeine, which is present in such small amounts that it's practically speaking impossible to get addicted to caffeine only by eating chocolate; and if you were, then drinking a coffee would make the 'chocolate craving' go away, which any 'chocoholic' will tell you isn't the case.

Psychological addictions also are usually the precursor to physical addictions in substances that are physically addictive. Methamphetamine (variously called *"meth"*, *"ice"*, *"P"* and several other street names) is a highly physically addictive substance; however statements that 'you get hooked from one puff' are totally untrue from a physical addiction perspective. The fact is that since methamphetamine makes the user feel great, in control, and powerful; people with self-confidence issues are likely to develop a strong psychological addiction almost immediately, and then through continued use develop a physical addiction.

Physical addictions are caused when the substance becomes a dependency in the body. There are two general actions that cause this to happen: either the drug takes the place of a natural substance, so the body stops producing the natural one; or the body produce more of something in order to block the drug or as a side-effect of the drug's action.

Either way, when the user stops taking the drug, their body or brain chemistry is now 'wrong' in that it's either not producing something that it needs; or is producing more of something that it no longer needs. Until such time as it works itself out, the user will suffer (sometimes powerful) negative effects of this imbalance. This is called 'withdrawal'.

Some psychological addictions contain a physical aspect; however, it is very minor. When you enjoy something greatly, your brain up-regulates the neurotransmitter dopamine, which makes you feel happy and gives a sense of accomplishment (as you will read in a later chapter, dopamine is associated with the brain's 'reward pathways').

Therefore, by missing out on the substance or activity, dopamine may be lower than your 'normal level' and this can lead to minor withdrawal effects such as listlessness, general negative feelings, and in extreme cases, minor clinical depression. Even the extreme case side of this however is extremely mild compared to the withdrawal from a drug that has caused a physical addiction. Plus of course, any activity that then up-regulates the dopamine again such as completing a task and being congratulated for a job well done; or other pleasurable activities will remove the craving and withdrawal symptoms immediately.

The most common physical addiction that many people are familiar with is that of cigarettes. Cigarettes contain a drug called nicotine, which takes most of the blame for the addiction, but it is actually a complex interaction of several different chemicals that leads to the physical addiction, including agents acting as MAOIs (monoamine oxidase inhibitor – a type of antidepressant). This is why quitting is so difficult for many people, as they experience multiple kinds of withdrawal simultaneously, including a withdrawal from an antidepressant after possibly years of use, which plays havoc with brain chemistry in general.

Coming back to LSD therefore, we need to consider both of these kinds of possible addiction. Firstly and easily, we will get physical addiction out of the way. LSD is not physically addictive at all. It does not cause any body or brain chemistry production to change. The affected parts of the brain – described later in more detail in the chapter "The Chemistry" – are affected to a large extent during the trip, but there are no natural chemicals that are produced more or less due to the LSD. There are therefore no withdrawal symptoms.

But, if it is such a powerful and profound experience, what about psychological addiction? If you take it and enjoy it so much, will you not want to use it again? Quite possibly, but not necessarily. The experience may be extremely positive, and I myself have definitely experienced cases where I have said to myself, "*I don't want this to end*" during a trip, or "*I really want to experience that again as soon as possible*" after a trip. As described in the introduction to this book, I have used LSD myself hundreds of times over the last fifteen to sixteen years of my life, and so it probably would not be unwarranted to say that at least psychologically speaking, I am in some way addicted. I would not however consider it to be a fair statement in general as the implication brought by such a statement does not truly reflect the reality of the situation.

Despite the possibility of making such statements yourself or having these kinds of feelings, there are several factors involved in the experience that will naturally cause you to regulate your use. As you have already read earlier, LSD generates a tolerance – if you have a wonderful trip and then want to try it again, you really can not do so for at least a week, unless you increase the dosage significantly. Simple availability and cost are going to prevent this relatively quickly.

Another factor is that not every trip is going to be a 'wonderful' experience. You will have trips that are amazing, and trips that are less than amazing. After a truly amazing experience, you may be tempted to try to re-create that feeling, but if the next trip isn't the same, your desire to try again in the short term will definitely be diminished.

Probably the strongest motivating factor in not tripping 'all the time' however is simply how powerful the experience is. As you have hopefully come to understand from this book so far, you need to be mentally prepared for a trip. After a powerful experience, you will almost certainly not feel 'up to it' to go through it again, even if it was an amazing and wonderful experience. If you do, then after your second trip in a short period of time, you will probably be so drained that the idea of doing it again anytime soon is likely to fill you with a sense of trepidation and dread.

Lastly, as mentioned, psychological addictions often have a physical component related to dopamine. As you'll read later about the chemistry and behaviour of LSD within the brain, there is no real opportunity for this to be a factor in an LSD experience as many of the relevant pathways within the brain are bypassed completely during the trip. The enjoyment itself is of a totally different kind to the 'dopamine rush' of other psychological addictions.

Quite simply, LSD is such a powerful experience that wanting to do it again soon is unlikely. Even if you were to do so and 'abuse' it, there is no action of physical addiction possible, including the physical (dopamine) aspects of psychological addiction.

You may – like me – end up in a situation where the experiences are profound, helpful and positive to the extent that LSD becomes an important part of your life. I could however decide today that I will never take LSD again and I would never experience any withdrawal or problems at all from doing so. I would miss it – because it is a beautiful and wonderful thing – but that is no different from missing friends and family that have passed away; or missing your childhood home. It is certainly not an addiction.

Don't Panic

I must not fear.
Fear is the mind-killer.
Fear is the little-death that brings total obliteration.
I will face my fear.
I will permit it to pass over me and through me.
And when it has gone past I will turn the inner eye to see its path.
Where the fear has gone there will be nothing.
Only I will remain.

Frank Herbert – Dune

In previous chapters, I have made some passing mention of uncomfortable, scary, or otherwise negative feelings when taking LSD. These are what are generally referred to as a 'bad trip', but the term 'difficult experience' is a much more accurate description. These are not a myth – they do happen – but if you know what to look out for and are correctly mentally prepared in advance as well as being in the right kind of environment ('set' and 'setting'), they most definitely can either be avoided or directed in such a way that positive gains are made from the negative experience.

The most common cause of bad trips is simply not being prepared for the experience. This happens when you expect it to be something other than what it is – for example, having used other non-psychedelic substances (or low-dose psychedelic usage) and expecting a similar experience; or not having used any kind of substance before, not knowing what to expect, and then not 'accepting' the trip as it happens.

Obviously if you are going to take LSD at some point in your life, there is going to be a first time. For your first time, you do not truly know what to expect no matter how much I or anyone else tries to tell you about it. Therefore, for your first trip, the most important thing to remember is to be open and accepting of the experience. The most important lesson I learned for avoiding difficult experiences – and especially on the first trip – is to simply 'let it happen'. Attempting to fight against it will usually fail. In some cases, especially towards the end of the trip, it is possible to learn to control the experience, but you have to accept that this may not work and should be prepared accordingly.

If and when a trip begins to become difficult for you, you need to know that it does not have to stay that way. Another common myth about 'bad trips' is that either the entire trip is 'good' or the entire trip is 'bad'. This is as nonsensical as saying that an entire holiday to the South of France was 'good' or the entire holiday was 'bad'. It may be, but in the vast majority of cases, there are good parts and bad parts – and the goal of the holiday, as well as your LSD trip, is to have as much 'good' as possible while minimising the 'bad' or at least getting something positive out of it.

My own first LSD experience, as you have read earlier, was quite horrific for a fairly large portion of the trip. I was completely unprepared in every way imaginable; but – self-evidently – there was at least enough in it to pique my interest and curiosity to the level that I wanted to try it again under more suitable circumstances.

There are two kinds of factors that can cause a trip to go bad: external influences – those related to your 'Setting'; and internal thoughts – those related to your 'Set'.

Assuming you have prepared your setting appropriately, external influences are usually not a concern. There are however always going to be external influences that you could not foresee and did not prepare for.

For example, this could be a young woman still living at home taking LSD in her room while her parents are away on holiday, only to have to deal with their unexpected early return. Or it could be a businessman getting a phone call from his office informing him of a stressful project that he immediately needs to take care of. Further still, it could be someone unexpectedly injuring themselves whilst wandering around outside and needing medical attention, so having to deal with the emergency room at the hospital whilst tripping. There are a myriad of things you can imagine as potential external influences that could happen outside of your control and carefully laid plans.

Sadly, there is not a lot that can be done at the time for dealing with these external influences if you were unable to prepare for them in some way beforehand. You simply need to ignore them as much as possible, telling yourself that you will deal with whatever it is when you are in a better state of mind for dealing with the real world.

From the examples, the young woman should tell her parents that she is very tired and wants to go to bed. The businessman should tell his office that he is dealing with some very important and difficult personal matters at the moment and will get to the project as soon as he can. Regardless of the situation, the goal is to get yourself away from the external influence and then put it out of your mind until later. For the injury, there is probably not much that can be done – but at least in most countries, doctor patient confidentiality should protect you if you choose to tell them the complete story.

Under no circumstances should you try to pretend that you are not tripping and then deal with the situation as you would normally. Simply put, you probably can not do so. You may feel as if you can – especially if you are still in the early stages of the trip – but as the trip becomes more powerful over time, it will become more and more difficult and the stress you put on yourself will only make the negative experience even worse and remove any real opportunity for useful introspection and self-discovery.

If your trip has been planned effectively, external influences are generally easy to avoid except for very rare cases. In the above examples, the young woman at home should have confirmed with her parents that they are still away before taking LSD; the businessman should have turned his phone off so that he could not be contacted; and for the person that was injured, greater care should have been taken in planning the trip's location to minimise the risk of injury through unsafe ground or so on. Again, not everything can be planned for – a badly sprained or twisted ankle that requires medical attention can happen to anyone who steps wrongly somewhere, even on flat ground and whether under the influence of LSD or not; and so of course there's no realistic way to plan for all such eventualities.

Assuming all external influences are under control as best they can be – as with the vast majority of trips that were prepared for correctly – the other type of thing that can cause a trip to be difficult is internal thoughts. These can also be prepared for, however it is an internal preparation rather than the perhaps more obvious external preparations.

The primary two internal thought processes that can be an issue are anxiety and panic. Both of these are caused by feelings of helplessness or of a loss of control. Additionally of course, often the former may lead to the latter. There are several possible causes, but as long as you know what to look out for, it is usually easy to avoid, or to steer yourself away from it when you find yourself beginning to experience it.

It is worth reiterating at this stage however that sometimes even negative experiences can have positive effects in the realm of self-discovery. This will be covered more in the following chapter; but for now, you can think of it as a learning experience. In the same way that being involved in a traumatic experience like a car accident can cause some people to come out with a new, positive outlook on life, negative experiences during a trip can have a similar effect. Of course, as you can also have positive effects from positive experiences, it makes sense to try to enjoy the trip as much as possible instead of allowing these darker feelings to occupy your mind all of the time.

The most common problem that I have seen people get themselves in to is attempting to organise or sort out the chaos that they have in their minds. This happens because most people are used to a certain level of order or structure in their lives. They mentally catalogue things, place them in to neat boxes, and then refer back to them later.

As discussed earlier, LSD weakens or removes the link between the input from the senses and the conceptual ideas that are placed on them. Relatedly therefore, it only makes sense that attempting to generate new conceptual ideas to put on to the experience is going to be doomed to failure. This is exactly what attempts to organise the chaos of the mind are doing – attempting to take all of the various pieces of input, put them in to neatly labelled boxes in the mind, and then put it aside as you would when in a 'normal' state of mind.

While you may be able to put the parts in to these mental boxes and even label them in some fashion, you can not put it aside for later – it's either there or it's gone. This however is the clue for solving the problem... it's either there or it's gone, so instead of having a mind full of labelled boxes and getting mentally buried under a mountain of half organised chaos, simply let it be gone. By trying to organise chaos instead of just letting it go by, you are only causing yourself stress and anxiety, as well as missing out on whatever new thoughts would flow in to your mind once you have let the old ones go. Trust in your ability to remember it later, and then afterwards – when the chaos is gone – you can organise it effortlessly.

So, as described, just let it happen. If the chaos is too much, do not try to organise it – just look at something else and see where that thing takes you. Alternatively, say to yourself – out loud if need be – "*Stop*" and then sit back, close your eyes if needed and relax. The chaos won't go away, but if you don't try to organise it, in a short time you'll find yourself starting to understand it without even trying; enjoying it; and possibly even beginning to learn something from it.

A related problem to this is a side effect of partial success in organising the chaos. I like to call this 'getting stuck in loops'. This is when you end up with circular reasoning on a thought or series of thoughts. You think about one thing, it leads to another, that to another, that to yet another and so on, however after a while you are at a thought that leads back to the first one.

These kinds of loops are not uncommon even in people who have not taken LSD. They can be frustrating when you realise you are not getting any further. Without LSD, you reach in to your mind and try to find new conceptual ideas that fit to the thoughts, hopefully leading you to a different pattern and out of the loop. Usually this works, and when it doesn't you just give up and move on to something else.

But with LSD, you have less access to your conceptual patterns to fit on to the thoughts. They are raw, unfiltered, and totally unlike any thoughts you are used to dealing with. So, you almost certainly will not succeed at getting yourself out with reasoning if you are stuck in a loop. The only solution is to simply give up.

In almost all cases that I have seen, people have been able to work themselves out of these issues with a minimum of difficulty and then gone on to experience a wonderful trip. But what if you can't? What if you try and fail?

If you believe that you will fail at doing this, you probably will. If you believe you can do it, you almost certainly can. Remember that what is happening is all inside your own mind. You mind is your own and despite how it may feel or seem at the time, does not have any external influences beyond the normal world outside of it – everything that is happening inside your mind is something you are creating yourself. Also, remember that later it will all make sense – anything you can not sort out now, just accept it and tell yourself you will sort it out later. Sit back, relax, and let it happen.

Another source of potential panic or fear is a change in the appreciation of size and scale. In normal day-to-day life, people adjust themselves to the size of the world they find themselves in – when you are driving along a road, you do not usually think about the fact that each building you pass has rooms, hallways, stairwells and so on. You know they do, but you do not contemplate that kind of size; it is just a building. It's only when you enter a building that the rooms become a solid reality to you and it all feels much larger than it did from outside. This is normal. But for most of us, it is only 'half true' on LSD. When outside, you may find yourself experiencing the absolute vastness of where you are; the 'inside perception' being used in an 'outside environment'. For me, there is always a sense of majesty and wonder at the universe when I see in this state how 'large' it appears to be. Some other people however find it difficult to manage and find themselves afraid of the vastness of it all.

Something that may help to deal with the vastness is a mental exercise that deliberately pictures this huge scale, but then puts it in to perspective. Picture a leaf. Then expand it out to a twig with a few leaves on it. Expand that out to a branch full of such twigs. Further out to a tree. Then a clump of trees. Keep the leaf in mind the whole time – how many there are. Then a forest. Then a continent covered in forests. Then the earth. Then the solar system. The galaxy. A cluster of galaxies. The universe. Zoom in on your mental image, all the way back to the leaf. That leaf is a part of this seemingly impossibly large universe; but it is still just a leaf. It is a wonder of nature and a miraculous beautiful thing – but were it a conscious being, it would be oblivious to the huge universe that it is a part of. It continues and survives without a care. It just is, and that is all it needs.

Doing this exercise not only helps you to get over any panic about the size and scale of everything, but even helps to gain a further appreciation of the scale in a positive way and lets you see the beauty and magic of the vastness rather than be terrified by it.

If absolutely necessary, there are a few tricks that might help against panic in general, but I certainly will not promise any of them are a golden bullet to solve the problem. The first is to increase external stimulus of some 'normal' things. Television, if you can at least half-way concentrate on it, makes a distraction that lessens the effect of a trip to an extent in some cases. This is also true for computer games that require focus; puzzles; and anything else that requires organisation outside of yourself and continued focus. These kinds of activities essentially force your mind to change to a different state, blocking out some of the LSD effect to a degree. That said, I do not recommend any of these. It may help, but it also means that you are hiding from your problem instead of facing it. Maybe you were just on the verge of learning something truly useful about yourself, and by hiding from it, you have lost any chance of that happening.

Medically speaking, there are also options for ending a trip prematurely. Generally speaking, this involves rendering the patient unconscious with specific kinds of sedatives or tranquilisers and so is obviously an extremely harsh – and usually completely unnecessary – solution to the perceived problem. It is also the case that in some early LSD experiments where the trip was to be ended early using these kinds of substances, they may simply have removed the person's ability to articulate that they were still experiencing the trip rather than actually ending it. To me, I can not imagine much worse than to be in such a fragile mental state and then have someone inject me with something that removes my ability to move and communicate.

It may theoretically be possible to dull the effects of the trip with some substances (e.g. alcohol) or to 'replace' the trip with a different state of mind using other substances (e.g. MDMA), but again I would not consider these to be productive, sensible, nor necessarily safe and can not advise it. No matter how harrowing or terrible the trip seems, you have the power within yourself to make it better. "Relax" is a much better choice than "pop a pill" or "deaden your mind".

Whilst writing this book, I had several LSD experiences, including one specifically for the purpose of recording my thoughts for the book itself. This was by far one of the least enjoyable trips I have had (although certainly not as bad as my first trip). I learned a lot from it and in general it was a positive experience for me, but it was nevertheless much darker and more harrowing than normal. There were many images in my mind that were much darker in tone and theme than usual and many thoughts that scared me on a fairly fundamental level. I believe the problem was quite simply that I was not 'letting the trip happen'; but instead I was trying to control it. I had to force myself to remain coherent enough to type it out as the trip happened, and then – when I couldn't manage that any longer – at least coherent enough to explain everything in my head to Lindsay so that she could type about it for me.

By forcing myself to do that, I had to fight against my own mind. This was a struggle that I can only assume would have led to a truly horrific bad trip if I were not already so familiar with the LSD experience. I felt so drained by the struggle though that by the end of the trip, I felt as though my mind had gone through a meat-grinder – not a headache as such, but rather just that everything was mashed, stretched and pulverised beyond recognition. I had lost a lot of myself in the fight and I did not have the energy to find those parts again that night.

This is however the first time since my first ever trip that I have had such strong negative feelings; and only for a part of it, as other parts of the trip I experienced euphoria, joy and wonderment as with every other trip. And the only reason I experienced the negativity was – perhaps ironically – because I was trying to understand it better by trying (only partially successfully) to keep it under control.

In the 1960s at the height of LSD's popularity, for a while it was not an uncommon occurrence for hospitals to be taking in young people experiencing 'bad trips'. This helped fuel many of the negative stories associated with LSD – after all, if so many people are ending up in hospital 'freaking out', then clearly the substance they used has a high risk potential for this happening, doesn't it?

In reality, there are three reasons to consider this to be blown out of proportion.

Firstly, the number of incidents was not as high as the media made out. This is purely and simply a case of propaganda as you will read more about in a later chapter. Out of the vast amount of users of LSD, the estimated figures calculate to less than one in ten thousand ever being admitted to a hospital during a difficult experience. As with anything, it is a numbers game – if someone says to you that one hundred people who took LSD were admitted to hospital, it sounds like a lot. But then if they mention to you that it is out of one million, the number suddenly seems far less significant.

Secondly, many people taken to hospital while on LSD did not begin to have a strongly negative experience ('freaking out' on the 'bad trip') until after the involvement of authorities. A group of young people on LSD attending a love-in may have all been fine. Then when the police arrived and started arresting people for drug possession, 'disorderly behaviour', or whatever else; the drastic change of the setting from one of peace and harmony to one of fear naturally causes some experiences to turn sour quickly. Or in other cases where the person was more passively taken away to a hospital, the bad trip began when they found themselves away from their friends, in an ugly sterile environment; and then compounded by being harshly strapped down to a bed with leather straps after they began to show initial signs of anxiety.

And lastly is more the fault of the people themselves. In this book, you are reading about how 'best' to experience an LSD trip – in the safest way possible whilst maximising enjoyment, self-discovery and consciousness expansion. Not everyone who comes across LSD is given this opportunity. Many – especially in the height of the popularity of the drug – would take it in extremely unsuitable environments, extremely unsuitable dosages, or both. Their 'set and setting' were wrong from the start and it's reasonable to expect that in such a scenario, the risk of a strongly negative experience is going to be much higher than for those using LSD with the right frame of mind and environment.

When an LSD trip is taken with the right frame of mind, in the right setting, and with enough mental preparation to be aware of the kinds of problems that you may face, the risk of the experience being overwhelmingly negative is extraordinarily slim. Every case of a bad experience that I have heard about has been related to the person's initial state of mind or expectations – their 'set' – or to their environment, whether the initial environment or one that was forced upon them later – their 'setting'.

The Multidisciplinary Association for Psychedelic Studies – better known as 'MAPS' – have a project called "*Zendo*". Zendo focuses on harm reduction by users of psychedelics, specifically in environments such as festivals and other locations where difficult trips may be experienced. Unlike traditional approaches to hospitalisation as mentioned above, Zendo provide an environment within the grounds of the festival where the person will feel comfortable and have access to talk to 'sitter' volunteers that are experienced and able to help the person that is in distress. In many cases, they are even able to help the tripper turn the difficult experience in to a learning experience where they gain real positive benefits.

If there is anything you take from this chapter, let it be that it is important to remember what I have said about suggestibility. If you hear that "*on LSD, you can have panic attacks*", you are more likely to have a panic attack. If you hear that *"on LSD, you see the walls melting"*, then this visual may predominate above others. This chapter has talked about some negative things that it is possible to experience, and so simply by having read about it, you may be more inclined to experience these things. I do apologise for that, but in deciding to write it, I weighed the pros and the cons and came up with the simple fact that it is better to know than not to know. Forewarned is forearmed. And, as mentioned earlier, simply knowing that this kind of suggestibility exists strongly reduces the chance of it influencing you.

Self-Discovery

"I got high on psychedelics before I was ever drunk. I never smoked. Then LSD came by. And to me it was the most wonderful thing that had ever happened... And, of course, the best drugs ever were manufactured by the government. ... LSD lets you in on something. When you're tripping, the idea of race disappears; the idea of sex disappears; you don't even know what species you are sometimes. And I don't know of anybody who hasn't come back from that being more humane, more thoughtful, more understanding."

Ken Kesey

Up to now, this book has focused on what LSD is, how it affects you, and practical advice for avoiding some potential problems during the experience.

The purpose of this chapter is somewhat different to the more practical chapters of before. Here, I want to discuss how best to make use of LSD to come away from the experience understanding more about yourself than you ever realised was possible going in to it.

This is in many ways the core of this book, as it is in fact the very reason why I myself have continued to use LSD all of these years.

Most likely, you are reading this book before you have ever taken LSD, and you are in fact a 'beginner'. Self-Discovery will begin to happen from your very first trip – possibly without you consciously needing to do anything to make it happen. Some of the techniques described in this chapter however may be too difficult for you until you have become accustomed to the LSD experience and can greet the experience comfortably as an old friend instead of a strange and confusing new one. That said however, there is nothing wrong with knowing about them now and considering how you might make use of them in future experiences if you are unable to do so during the first time. Self-Discovery is a process that – with or without psychedelic substances – takes time.

LSD is not magical. You can not just take LSD and suddenly expect that the next day you will automatically be wiser, happier, and better than you were before. These changes are things that happen to a person over time, within themselves – LSD facilitates these changes by changing how you perceive the world, but does not directly cause the changes itself.

The psychedelic researcher, Professor Doctor Torsten Passie, described it to me with a metaphor. You are on a ship, perhaps even the captain of that ship, sailing the high ocean. Somewhere on the vast and mostly empty ocean is an island; and on this island is treasure. You do not know where the island is, and you have been sailing for a long time now. After a while, many people begin to give up hope. Maybe the treasure is a lie; maybe there is no island – just ocean forever. They become despondent and stop searching. Taking LSD is like getting in a helicopter, flying to the island, seeing the treasure, and then flying back to your ship. You still don't have it; but now you *know* it's real. You *know* it's there. And you *know* you can get to it. This is a very powerful motivator.

The way in which you decide to prioritise your trust in how you experience the world can also be altered quite significantly. Imagine you are walking down the street and suddenly, out of the corner of your eye, you find you notice – just for a moment – a giant green bug-eyed alien. What you believe based on this varies from person to person. Some people will believe that giant green bug-eyed aliens exist – after all, they just saw one. Others may believe they have been slipped a hallucinogenic drug (however, as stated, this kind of 'hallucination' will not happen; so only those who have never taken one will be likely to believe this). Yet others still may believe they have gone mad, or are asleep and dreaming. And others still may simply believe that the alien they saw is a very convincing fake.

Before I had ever taken LSD, I completely trusted my senses. I believed that if I saw something, it was there. I probably would have leaned towards believing that the bug-eyed alien was a very convincing fake. However now I am more aware that my senses are just my viewport to reality – they are not reality itself.

They can be wrong, and in fact often are. I have seen the world unfiltered and now know how much there is in day to day life that we do not see, or interpret differently to the truth. Were I to get a glimpse of that alien today, my reaction would be to dismiss it as a false interpretation of reality – an illusion created by my mind from an incomplete glance at something that is most likely much more mundane.

The first time my wife, Lindsay, took LSD we took only a relatively small dose – around 75µg to 100µg. I had expected quite a strong effect on her, however after 90 minutes, she reported that she really was not feeling anything and wanted to go to bed. I was shocked, as I was feeling the effects – not strongly – but definitely there. I thought perhaps that maybe the LSD I had had somehow become damaged at the edges of the square of blotter tabs that I had and she had perhaps taken one of those edge pieces. We went to bed, and then finally the effects slowly began to come on for her. We laughed and enjoyed ourselves for several hours talking about all of the things in our minds. Then, after making love (as described earlier in this book), we talked a little more about some very honest and personal subjects, then lay quietly for a while and just followed through our own thoughts until sleep finally took us quite some time later.

The next day, she told me about some of the things in her mind from the night.

As I have mentioned, Lindsay is German and has had a significantly more sheltered life than I have. Since knowing me, and my friend Sebastian, she has begun to take note of how much we talk about Germans – as a general cultural norm – as being reserved, held-back, structured and organised. I believe she sees many of these traits in herself.

She told me of a cartoon world that represents her inner self. The cartoon is a simple, child-like cartoon world – not like the Manga style of cartoon that she prefers on television. In this world, there is a basement, containing a chest. The room itself is like an extremely large box. In the corners of the room there are baby devils with the German flag both in the background behind the devils and on the devils' skin themselves – black face and upper chest; red midsection and gold below; however the gold is hard to see and not clear or bright. Wrapped around the chest is a chain with a lock – all as cartoons, large and unrealistic. On the chest sits Lindsay herself – not a cartoon, but real. The chest can not be opened as long as she is sitting there. This locked chest represents her inhibitions; her hidden feelings and emotions are inside. She can not let them out – she won't let herself – and the devils are watching.

The symbolism here is of course so obvious that I hardly need to explain it further. I only hope that over time she thinks about this chest, and what it might take to open it.

This leads to the first technique that I recommend for directed self-discovery. If you encounter such an image in your mind, you should try to change it. For Lindsay, she wasn't ready, but next time she sees this world, I want her to picture a key unlocking the padlock; getting up off the chest; defying those devils and opening the chest. Maybe she can do it, maybe she can't. Maybe she doesn't even know what is in the chest, or maybe when she sees what it is, it still won't be clear or obvious to her and she will need to work more on figuring that out. But these are all questions for later – first she needs to try to open the chest.

Even without having opened it however, Lindsay has learned something about herself. She's learned that the inhibitions are there in a more real fashion than she might have previously known; she's learned at least part of what it is that stops her reaching in to those parts of her self; and she's learned what it is to see herself from outside as an objective observer instead of only the perspective from within.

Thinking about her cartoon world from another somewhat more light-hearted angle, Lindsay felt as if maybe she better understood the humour of some simpler forms of cartoon – The Powerpuff Girls™, Roadrunner and Coyote, and so on; the types of cartoon that she'd never normally enjoy.

Thus far, we have not yet tried watching any such cartoons together, but I would be interested to find out if she can retain the childlike wonder and appreciation that this style of humour aims at. I think perhaps that like many people, she represses aspects of herself that she views as childlike or inappropriate. If she can open herself up to laugh at absurdity and enjoy some of the more simple things in life, it would be a great improvement for her life.

Further in Lindsay's cartoon world, but beyond the room itself, there were other people, who also appeared 'real' rather than cartoons. These people had tattoos, which moved and shifted in the same way as the simple 'shifting' visual effects that LSD produces. She found it unpleasant.

I am not really sure what to make of this myself, and Lindsay couldn't tell me either when I questioned her about it the next day. She simply said that that is what was there and that she did not like it.

At one point in the night, Lindsay spent some time practicing some directed visualisation. Instead of simply letting her imagination come up with imagery, she tried to create some imagery of her own. It worked surprisingly well. She built us both out of candy in her mind. She had peppermint skin, chocolate blood, and hair out of sage flavoured hard-boiled candies. She built me out of full-milk chocolate with white peppermint over it; my moustache and small beard were made out of strings of a sweet liquorice sauce.

This kind of directed mental visualisation can be just a little bit of fun, as I suspect Lindsay was having when doing it; but it can also be a useful tool for self-discovery. It is a skill that – with practice – allows you to take control of the less-directed visualisations that occur. If Lindsay had done this prior to the room with the chest, it is possible that creating a key and using it on the lock may have been easier for her.

Lindsay, like many women, has an irrational fear of insects. She surprised herself when she felt as if there were insects crawling on her skin and it was somehow a positive and nice feeling rather than negative.

I must say that I am quite unsure what to make of this – sadly, I am not a psychoanalyst, simply someone with an interest in how the mind works. It definitely seems positive as it may represent a burgeoning realisation that there truly is in fact nothing to be afraid of with insects; however as it was a feeling only and not something that she pictured in her mind, it may also simply be the feeling of a light touch as being pleasant.

Another thought that went through her head concerned a view of herself; perhaps her wish or goal for a better, improved self. "Angel or dragon?" The angel was perfect – clean and white, with nothing out of place. But the dragon... dragons are more defined. They are not perfect, but they do not have to be.

They have self-confidence, and can even be physically ugly, but have beauty that comes from their strength, power and might. It is irrelevant to a dragon what other people think of it.

Lindsay gained a lot of weight after the birth of our daughter and has had some trouble losing it. This has led to some – but thankfully not too many – self-confidence issues. I believe the thoughts with the angel or dragon was her way of being more accepting of her outer self and understanding that by working on her inner self and not caring so much about the opinions of others, she can resolve the issues. Being either the angel or the dragon would be a solution; but the dragon is something she can become, while no person can ever be the perfect angel no matter how hard they try.

Some experiences with self-discovery can be positive feelings, even when showing you negative things. This is how it's always been for myself – even when I learn things about myself that I don't like, it's always framed in my mind in a way that I can say, *"okay, I see that now – it isn't good, and I can change it"*. However, even quite negative experiences can be extremely helpful.

I have heard a first-hand story of someone who has taken psychedelics on many occasions. He found that on many trips, he was outside, looking in on himself – not an uncommon experience in and of itself – however he could see all of his imperfections much more clearly; all the things that made him not as good as he could otherwise have been stood out glaringly. Instead of it being an immediate learning experience, it caused him anxiety and suffering for the period of the trip, realising that he was nowhere near as good as he could be.

But he used this experience to better himself. Every time he saw his imperfections, he was able to use this to correct them after the trip was over. The trips were not telling him he needed to be perfect. He did not feel he needed to be like a guru, or a god. He only realised they were telling him, "*You have the potential to behave in another way, and you should do that.*"

Every time he improved and got closer to his true potential, the psychedelic trips he took became less uncomfortable for him until he was finally much closer to the 'best' version of himself that he could picture himself being.

My own experiences with self-discovery and improvement are something I had a hard time defining in the pages of this book. I never experienced any great revelation that I could immediately take something away from and improve myself with. Nevertheless, I have experienced a great deal of 'smaller' revelations that have allowed me to grow as a person far beyond what I was before. Complicating matters is that, as mentioned in the introduction of this book, I have Asperger's Syndrome. This means that my specific experiences are likely not as easy to relate to for most people. That said however, I think it is possible that at least for some of my experiences, some people will be able to relate to some degree or other.

A good example of this is how I interact with other people. One of the major aspects of Asperger's is difficulty reading other people's emotions and reacting accordingly – quite simply, we don't have the automatic recognition of things like facial expressions or body stance that others do and so we learn to 'read' expressions manually instead of doing it instinctually.

To me, growing up, there was very little difference between a tree and a person in how I saw and 'automatically' valued them.

When most people look at a scene containing four trees and one person, their focus will automatically be on the person. When I look at the same scene there is around a one in five chance I will focus on the person (until they move or do something). My brain just does not register that the person shape has any kind of special status over the tree shapes.

I know of course, intellectually speaking, that the person is more interesting than any of the trees. So it makes sense to focus on the person instead of them. This was obvious to me even as a child, however if I did not notice the fact that there was a person there, then I could hardly be blamed for focusing on a tree instead.

What changed for me with LSD however is that I realised how to take in a full picture and then devote my attention to the appropriate thing much more quickly. When on LSD, the conceptual ideas are broken down and so there can be no innate sense of focus (whether you have Asperger's or not). This forced me to learn a new way to develop and concentrate my focus, which I can use in day-to-day life. Now, when I look at a scene, I don't just focus on the first thing to grab my attention, but instead I take in the whole scene. I see everything and then can intellectually decide, *"yes, the person is the most valuable thing in the scene to get my attention"* and so they do. I still can not – and probably never will – be able to focus on the person instinctually, but I can certainly 'fake' it better now than I ever could before I had LSD.

Another aspect is panic. I feel uncomfortable in crowded situations – any time there are a lot of people around, there is so much chaos around me that it becomes difficult for me to think clearly. This was especially bad when I was younger. In my early twenties, simply visiting a supermarket at the wrong time of day would be enough to lead to a panic attack. LSD has greatly helped me to accept chaos and be less concerned about it. These days, I still feel uncomfortable in large crowds; however, I have not had a panic attack in over ten years.

These two things were both significant changes in my life that I attribute to the experiences I had thanks to LSD. However, they both pale in comparison to the largest and most significant changes – learning to accept things and prioritising my life.

Like most people – or so I am told – I had a fear of death. Most of the time it was a niggling little thought in the back of my mind that I would blot out as being too uncomfortable to think about; but other times it would keep me awake at night and in dark times in my life could even bring me to tears. As an atheist, I have no comfort of belief in an afterlife – my belief is that when you are dead, you are gone. It's not 'blackness', it's just 'gone'. After you are dead, it is just the same as before you were born, there is no 'you' anymore. The 'you' two hundred years from now (barring advances in medical science) is the exact same 'you' that existed two hundred years ago. You did not exist, and you will not exist.

I could always intellectually understand and accept that based on these beliefs, I should have nothing to fear. After I am dead, there is no 'me' anymore to have any feelings – good or bad – and so fearing it is pointless. Despite this intellectual understanding, I still feared it, for no fathomable reason that I can explain – it was a simple, basic terror.

One day, during the height of an LSD trip, I was thinking about death. It took me a little while to realise that – contrary to normal – I was not afraid. The logical intellectual reasoning suddenly made sense to me on an emotional level as well – there was no need to continue fearing it, just live my life, one day die, and that's it. The next day, I was even more surprised to think about it briefly as I lay in bed, and again feel no fear. It was then I realised that intellectually minded or not, the intellectual reasoning alone was never enough, I had to really 'accept' it, and now I finally did.

I certainly do not want to die, and I worry about what would happen to my family were I to be killed in a car accident; but it no longer preoccupies my thoughts at night. I no longer cry myself to sleep over the inevitable. I live my life more fully and happily, without always asking myself, "what's the point? I'll be dead one day anyway."

Beyond accepting death, I have also learned – in similar ways – to accept many other things. Overall, I would say I have become an extremely tolerant person. When someone criticises my work, I can now ask them what they think I can do to improve it, without feeling hurt or angry at their criticism. When I have an appointment to do something I do not want to do, I no longer pine and mope over the lost time (which only wastes more time anyway) – I just get it done and out of the way as quickly as I can.

Don't get me wrong – I haven't achieved some kind of 'nirvana'. I still gripe about things that annoy me from time to time; I still get stressed at work when there is a lot on my plate; I still have good days and bad days just like anyone else. But I handle it better now. It is just a change in my mind-set about how to deal with things that are outside of my control – to accept them.

Not all aspects of self-discovery that LSD brings on are necessarily immediately positive. Learning things about yourself can sometimes show you things that are negative, but beyond that, it can also show you things that you view as positive, but have a somewhat negative effect when you go to act on them. I personally describe this as a positive thing; however, it won't always appear to be such for an outsider.

For me, such a thing is the other side of the coin to 'acceptance'. While I am more able to accept things some things, I am less able to accept others. As described, I no longer accept wasting time unnecessarily. Nor do I accept related things such as spending my time watching someone do something the wrong way – I need to either help them do it the right way (or at least better), or get out and do something else. The former is often construed as unwanted help and the latter is often construed as impolite.

Recently, I have begun deliberately pushing some of my own boundaries on LSD as a kind of self-experimentation. I have been curious to test my own feelings under different circumstances; most especially circumstances in which I am uncomfortable or unsure of my feelings.

This is not something I would recommend for a beginner to LSD – before you begin to push boundaries, it is first important to become comfortable and somewhat familiar with the normal experience of the psychedelic state of mind.

One example of this is crowded situations. I feel uncomfortable in crowds when not on LSD and it is quite normal for almost anyone to feel uncomfortable in crowds when on LSD. So for me, being on LSD in crowded situations was one of the worst things I could imagine.

Around a year before I began writing this book, I experienced an LSD trip and began thinking about this. I decided I want to figure out why I feel uncomfortable in crowds. What is it about the situation that causes me stress and discomfort?

So, some time later, when I felt I would be ready for it, I took another LSD trip where I deliberately exposed myself to the 'edge' of such a situation – not in the middle of it, and with an easy escape route if I needed it. As I expected, I quickly began to feel very uncomfortable and out of place. What I did then however was different – instead of 'getting away' as I normally would, I 'detached myself' from the part of my mind that was experiencing this anxiety and objectively analysed it. Why was it uncomfortable? What was the trigger?

What I learned from doing that is that my discomfort was caused by a kind of fear. I feared the possibility of having to interact with the people, which appeared to be self-evidently greater in a crowd than not in a crowd. I analysed this thought further and came to the conclusion that while a crowd does present a higher possibility of interaction than a place completely devoid of people, it is actually significantly lower than the possibility of interaction in a place with only a few people. This comforted me to an extent.

But that was not enough. I wanted to delve deeper in to the causes. I now understood the anxiety in crowds was based on a fear of interaction, so my next step was to determine why interaction was something that I wanted to avoid. On this trip, I could not bring myself to attempt interaction with people (other than friends tripping with me of course), so decided to save the idea for a later trip.

Some months later, I had an opportunity for another trip in a kind of party environment where I knew there would be many people, but I should be able to get out quite easily. This was the situation I had been waiting for.

I prepared some aspects of the environment carefully. People that would be there who I knew well, but weren't sure if they'd be 'accepting' of me on LSD in front of them, I gave prior warning by telling them – quite directly – that I planned to take LSD that evening. For some of them, this was quite a shock, but for some others it generated a kind of interest in what I was doing. Some others seemed to be uncomfortable with the idea and spent the entire night avoiding me.

Despite this, there were of course very many people there who had no idea that I had taken LSD. I spent the majority of the evening standing at a table with the people I felt the most comfortable around. Several times throughout the night, I was approached by other people and had to interact with them as one expects in that kind of environment. Some of the people that I decided I could trust, I told that I had taken LSD. This generated yet more shock from some, but generally, the reaction was positive more than negative; and the 'worst cases' were overall fairly neutral. One of the most positive reactions by far was an in-depth discussion about LSD, the effects and so on. That person also expressed an interest in this book when I told him about it and was the recipient of several draft versions prior to publication.

The people that approached me that I did not tell I had taken LSD were by far the most interesting (and difficult) for me. One person asked why I wasn't drinking alcohol and the best answer I could give him was *"personal reasons"*. As far as I could tell however, he did not seem to be aware that I was not in a 'normal' state of mind.

Unfortunately, while I think it was an interesting experience despite being quite uncomfortable at times, I frustratingly did not learn any further about what it is that causes my fear of interaction. I think I came close at times, but the discomfort itself – combined with the noisy and busy environment – was distracting me from the kind of self-analysis that I wanted to do. I therefore intend to repeat the experiment again if I can find an appropriate situation where this kind of interaction is needed but with less noise and chaos around me.

LSD and Creativity

"It's a psychic energizer... It releases the subconscious. It makes you see all your guilts, fears, repressions and insecurities. It makes you free."

Cary Grant

Beyond self-discovery alone, LSD provides opportunities for the enhancement of creativity – possibly directly whilst experiencing a trip – but usually more often than not, afterwards. This is because of the way that it changes how you think about things. This is most noticeable by virtue of changing how you perceive things, but it goes beyond that.

For myself, I have often made use of my LSD experiences for creativity, both during the trip and afterwards. As yet, I haven't come up with any truly great works or ideas[1] – and I may never do so – however I attribute a great deal of the quality of the software I write in my day job to the influence of LSD as well as my general approach of creatively solving everyday problems in my day to day life.

Aldous Huxley once described the psychedelic experience as being that normally when you look at things, your eyes and mind are preoccupied with the spatial dimensions – where things are, how big they are, and how they relate to other things. When using psychedelics, the ability to determine those things is not particularly diminished, but rather their importance is. What has become important in place of these things is intensity of existence, profundity of significance, and relationships within a pattern. To put it more simply, the 'being' and 'meaning' trump the 'measures' and 'location'.

What this means for creativity is many faceted. The creative process can be summed up as one of deriving novel thoughts from known information. You start with – as in any endeavour –

---

[1] I'm not quite vain enough to refer to this book as a 'great work'

only what you already know or can learn; and you end up with something new that did not exist before. Quite simply therefore, having a new way of looking at things provides you with a wealth of new information that can be used and applied to the creative process.

Beyond this, because the natural filters are broken down, you have the opportunity to use your modified perception to think about or visualise things in new ways that might never have occurred to you before – with altered perception comes altered outcomes.

Often, despite your enhanced creative thinking, you will find that actually performing creative activities is significantly more difficult and less appealing than you might have assumed. This is of course different for everyone and if you find yourself able and willing to actually perform a creative task, there is no good reason not to do so. In the case of a musician composing, a writer writing, a programmer programming, an artist painting or so on; I would however always recommend re-checking the work the following day.

This is probably especially true for the arts that directly affect the senses rather than reasoning – that is, music, painting, sculpture, and so on. Because your own sense for how something sounds is significantly altered when on LSD, it may be possible for a musician to create music that is enjoyable for other people also on LSD, but creating music that is enjoyable for people in general may be more difficult. You might create what is in actuality a masterpiece, but discard it as 'bland' or 'boring'; or you might create what sounds like the most magical harmony to you only to find the next day that the complexity and detail you heard when you wrote it is actually lost in a cacophony of noise to the 'normal' ear.

Many famous musicians however are known for their use of LSD – perhaps none better than The Beatles. The name and lyrics of the song *"Lucy in the Sky with Diamonds"* are often debated as to whether it is an 'LSD song' or not, but even if it wasn't intended as such, it's hard to believe the musical sound and psychedelic imagery weren't at least somewhat inspired by the LSD experiences that they had had.

Some other Beatles songs, such as *"Come Together"*, *"Strawberry Fields Forever"*, and *"Tomorrow Never Knows"* are much more openly 'LSD songs' and the members of the band were usually not shy to talk about their experiences with LSD. Paul McCartney – usually the most reserved about the topic of psychedelics compared to the rest of the band – is famously quoted as saying of LSD, *"It opened my eyes and made me a better, more honest, more tolerant member of society."*

For other kinds of creative tasks – those that are not purely sensory – the greatest problem is somewhat different: that of having to follow the 'rules'. Computer programming is such an art in that it is an art built out of a defined science. Computer science dictates how computers function; and programming languages are representations of how a programmer tells the computer to do what he wants it to do. The art for a programmer comes in the creation of software that does things in the way he wants it to do it – it has his own unique style; the user interface represents his vision; and the code itself may have an elegant flow to it that other programmers can recognise and admire. But, at its heart, the program code itself is still based on a strictly defined set of rules. Failing to keep to these rules will not create a 'worse piece of software'; it simply will not create a piece of software at all.

Following the 'rules' of any creative process where that process has such defined rules can be difficult whilst experiencing an LSD trip. The reason for this is that these kinds of rules especially are based on conceptual ideas, and it is these very same conceptual ideas that you are deliberately throwing away when you take psychedelics. The very thing that makes the experience so powerful for helping you to be creative by thinking about things in new ways is the same thing that makes the experience so uniquely unsuitable for following defined rules and structures.

That said however, it is not a wasted endeavour. As LSD does not affect memory, you can hold on to the creative ideas that require rules and use them later when the trip is over. Creative ideas that do not require rules or those that you think you are still capable of following due to the rules being quite simple, you can happily begin to do at any time during the trip – and I encourage you to do so if the impulse strikes.

This kind of creativity is of course seen most with people in the artistic fields and if you look at famous artists throughout history, you'll find a significantly higher proportion of psychedelic use than amongst the mainstream population or even 'celebrities' outside of the artistic fields. That does not mean however that art is the only field of creativity that LSD can positively influence – it is simply perhaps the most obvious.

Beyond the artistic realm, creativity is something that almost every person demonstrates every day of their lives. Whenever you have a new problem that you have not previously encountered and need to come up with a solution, there is some kind of creativity involved. This can even be as something as day-to-day as deciding on a new and interesting dinner instead of making the same old thing yet again that you are getting a bit tired with.

Even this kind of creativity is influenced by LSD. I learned to cook at school and also from my mother. When I first left home and lived on my own however, I had no motivation or interest to try new things – it was 'simpler' to just make the same kind of thing all of the time. I certainly did get bored with it, but even the boredom was not sufficient motivation to make me want to try other things. This all began to change after I started taking LSD however. I never had a moment during a trip where I said, *"Hey, maybe I'll make something interesting to eat!"* – just that when not tripping, I found I had become more curious and experimental. I simply had more motivation to try out new ideas in the kitchen. Cooking and baking interesting foods are now two things that I really enjoy and I happily experiment with creative new ideas regularly (much to the delight of my wife and daughter).

I have heard very many similar stories of improved creativity from others as well. Both as general creative improvements like my cooking, and as spontaneous decisions to change creative focus. From a mechanic who became interested in robotics after visualising the circuitry in his head during an LSD trip; through to a marketing executive who quit his high-paying job that made him miserable to become a graphic designer at significantly less pay, but a lot more personal satisfaction.

Perhaps one of the most significant studies for showing the creative benefit of psychedelics was performed in 1966 – it was called 'Psychedelics in Problem Solving' and was conducted by the 'International Foundation for Advanced Studies' also known as 'IFAS'. The study was unfortunately cut short with no opportunity for further on-going studies due to the ban on psychedelics taking effect the very same day that the substance was administered to the volunteers for the first (and only) main experiment.

Despite being cut short, the study showed some very interesting results.

Prior to the main round of the experiment, a preliminary experiment was done with two groups of four people. One of these groups received 50µg of LSD each and the other received 100mg of mescaline[1] each. They were then asked to work on problems assigned by the researchers. Both groups showed potential positive creativity in these tasks, however (according to the researcher) the lack of personal investment in the tasks – that is to say, the fact that they didn't really care about what they were assigned to do – negatively affected the actual production of any results.

For the main experiment itself, twenty seven volunteers from a variety of professional careers that require creative thought were given 200mg of mescaline and allowed to work on a pre-chosen problem from their own profession that they had been working on for at least three months, but had failed to solve as yet. This was done so that the participants were more personally invested in solving the problem as had been determined to be a negative factor in the preliminary experiment.

----

[1] Mescaline is a psychedelic with very similar, however not identical, properties and effects to LSD; this dosage of 100mg is considered very light – roughly equivalent to the 50µg of LSD received by the first group.

Six weeks later, the subjects reported back. At least twelve of the twenty seven volunteers had either solved their problem or come significantly further in the development of the ideas. Their reports also included sufficient information to determine that the improvements to creativity lasted significantly longer than the effects of the psychedelic substance itself. Several of the solutions that were found were in highly technical fields and were sufficiently novel and useful to be considered significant enhancements in the study of the science. This included a mathematical theorem regarding 'NOR gates[1]'; a design for space probe experiments for measuring properties of the sun; and insights in to the use of interferometry in a specific field of medicine.

Had this experiment been allowed to continue with repeated tests on more subjects, a wider range of professions with different types of problems to solve, and further tests with different kinds of psychedelic substances such as LSD; we would almost certainly know a very great deal more about creativity than we now do – as well as having even more practical results as with the above!

Another side effect of having additional creativity is spontaneously coming up with novel ideas about the universe in general; especially if you are inclined – as many are on LSD – to consider the 'big picture' of the universe and all that it entails. As I am a scientifically minded person – or at least like to

------

[1] 'NOR gates' are a type of logic gate, very important in the study of computer science, electronics and other such cases where mathematical logic is practically applied.

consider myself as such – I am always very careful to label my assumptions as such and logical conclusions as being dependent on these assumptions. This is even the case when on a trip, as LSD has absolutely no effect on this part of the reasoning process.

Less scientifically minded people certainly will not be any less creative in their ideas about existence, being and the universe, however their ideas may come out less scientifically sound, just as they would in other situation where they spontaneously come up with ideas. Depending on your own personal views with regards to science, the universe and possibly religious beliefs however, that may or may not necessarily be a problem for you.

One such idea that I spontaneously had – born almost fully formed in a 'flash' of inspiration under the influence of LSD and then developed and refined further in pieces both with and without LSD – was about an idea regarding consciousness and randomness in an infinite universe.

The idea can be summed up roughly as follows:

Assumption 1: *Existence is infinite in either time, space or both.*

The universe appears to have had a definite beginning and a physical size with limits. This at first glance makes it seem that existence is not infinite. However, while we can posit a (possible) start for the universe, we are not sure an end can be posited. Also, the 'start' has often been considered the start of the 'measurable' universe – that is, there is something that can be said to come 'before', but due to the nature of the big bang, it is impossible (and therefore meaningless within traditional physics) to talk about what happened 'before'. Additionally, I am using the term 'before' fairly loosely, as time as we know it appears to be a property formed by our universe anyway. However, ideas such as M-Theory posit 'brane' collisions as a possible 'universe starting event'; and of course there are also many other ideas, including the random creation of a particle and anti-particle annihilating (see assumption 2).

Assumption 2: Randomness exists in the universe.

We believe that thermodynamics can not be violated – matter and energy can neither be created nor destroyed, only change form. However interestingly, it is not against this rule for particles and anti-particles to spontaneously form, since the net energy result of this is still absolutely zero. We believe this may in fact be happening all throughout the universe quite a lot (there is reasonably strong evidence for this). Within the universe itself, there are very few real effects of this that we know of, however these microscopic events could – through the butterfly effect – in theory lead to larger real effects. Additionally, if there was 'nothing' at the time this happens, then this would (also in theory) be enough to kick-start a universe (see assumption 1).

Beyond spontaneous random particle creation, quantum physics points to the idea that many aspects of the universe are in fact based purely on probability of outcomes rather than definite outcomes.

Assumption 3: Consciousness – our sense of self – is a by-product of the way our brains organise data and has no reliance on a soul or any other external influence.

The patterning that creates consciousness is within our brains, however conceivably could form in anything (flows of hydrogen within a star easily rival the complexity of our brains for example)

Conclusion: *In an infinite universe, where randomness exists, any pattern conceivable must eventually form; and will do so forever (forms; gets destroyed; forms again; etc.). Therefore, the consciousness that we currently experience must eventually re-form somewhere/sometime else in the future. It may have already also done so many times in the past (although this is not guaranteed). When it re-forms, most iterations of it will not remember the previous (there is no definitive need for it to do so) and therefore will not realise it is a repeat of a previous consciousness. However, purely by chance (remembering: infinite universe and randomness) it must eventually also form with all previous memories intact. While you will be dead, the consciousness that you experience with all memories of being you, will continue. This arguably is indistinguishable from 'you' existing again in the same way that there is no definitive way you can prove (even to yourself) that you are in fact the same person as five minutes ago rather than being an exact copy that happens to have all the same memories.*

That said of course, it must eventually also form with a bunch of memories that have not previously happened; and indeed also with memories of things that happened to other consciousnesses. This is the nature of randomness.

Not conclusions: *This does not explain reincarnation; past life experiences; or anything else like that. They may seem related, but they are not. They are simply aspects of your current existing consciousness.*

It is worth pointing out that I do not necessarily believe this to be true, but rather simply that the conclusions reached are logical given that the assumptions presented are true. Should any of the assumptions turn out to be false, the conclusion becomes nothing more than a meaningless thought experiment.

I am okay with that, because that is how science works – a hypothesis is presented, tested and then falsified in favour of a better one. I presented the idea in this book not to try to convince you of the reality of the rebirth of consciousnesses (as said, I don't necessarily subscribe to it being true); but rather to give an idea of how minds – or at the very least *my* mind – can be influenced by LSD to creatively and quite spontaneously come up with a complex idea without deliberately spending any effort on the process.

A more famous – and much more practical – example of creativity in the sciences is that of the Polymerase Chain Reaction method, also known as PCR. The biochemist Dr Kary Mullis won the Nobel Prize for his work in creating PCR, which allows amplification of strands of DNA, generating potentially millions of strands from just a few. The process is used now with extreme regularity in any case where DNA is studied or analysed. Without it, we would have nowhere near the understanding of DNA that we do today. With regard to his invention, Dr Mullis is well known for having said, *"What if I had not taken LSD ever; would I have still invented PCR? I don't know. I doubt it. I seriously doubt it."*

Creativity is a nebulous concept. There is the direct idea of creating something new that wasn't there before; but to create something differently – in a better way than existed before – is also a creative process and indeed no less of one than the generation of something totally new.

The co-founder and former CEO of Apple, Steve Jobs, used LSD many times in his younger days (at least...) and was not shy to attribute a lot of the creativity he put in to his company to his experiences. *"Taking LSD was a profound experience, one of the most important things in my life. LSD shows you that there's another side to the coin, and you can't remember it when it wears off, but you know it. It reinforced my sense of what was important – creating great things instead of making money, putting things back into the stream of history and of human consciousness as much as I could."*

Next time you are using an iPhone, iPad, Mac computer or other Apple product, stop a moment to pay attention to the complete design package. For the most part, the hardware and software work smoothly together without the user having to consider anything special; the software components interact according to a typical user's expectations. Overall, it 'just works'[1]. Steve Jobs was famous for how strict he was as a CEO about these kinds of aspects of the products Apple produces, and it seems clear that this vision was inspired in no small part by the psychedelic experiences that he had with LSD.

To relate one such experience of my own: I was having difficulty designing a user interface for a complex piece of software. Due to the complexity and amount of configurability added throughout the last few versions, the user interface had

---

[1] As a software developer, I can honestly say I'm not actually a huge fan of many Apple's products, as the same thing that makes for a great user experience is often constricting to a highly technical person; but I accept the reasoning and trade-off as being the 'right thing' for them to have done.

grown in to quite a monstrosity of checkboxes, tabs with sub-tabs, text entry fields and so on. All of this configured a text file that advanced users could configure by hand if they felt comfortable doing so, however for the users that prefer a graphical option for configuration, I was quite aware that my software was less than user friendly. After having spent all of a Friday working on different layout designs and not really being happy with any of them, I finished work for the day then went out with a friend to a park and took LSD with him.

I had no intention of thinking about work any further at the time and really just wanted to leave it for Monday. Then, at one point during the trip, I looked at a small bridge over a river, and suddenly the user interface design was clear to me. The bridge was formed out of a series of triangles creating support structures and I immediately related this to a hierarchy of settings. In my mind, each category of settings fit itself in to the metalwork of the bridge and I could place the settings themselves within the hierarchy. On the following Monday, I implemented the new user interface design and after it was released, I received praise from the users at how intuitive and clear the configuration in the new version was compared to the old one.

In the previous chapter, I discussed the concept of self-discovery at some length. Self-discovery is a process, not a result. The result of 'self-discovery' is of course greater 'self-awareness'. Without too much mental exercise, it should be quite clear that improved self-awareness leads directly to improved creativity in and of itself.

Basically put, when you understand more about 'who you are', a natural side-effect is a better understanding of 'what you can do' and 'how you can do it'. By knowing both your strengths and your weaknesses, you are better able to channel creative efforts in valuable directions instead of reaching road-blocks that are above your current knowledge and skill level; or alternatively not investigating avenues that you might have been able to tackle by assuming them to be too difficult.

A simple example of this improvement to creativity from self-awareness is in your hands right now. Had I never taken LSD, it is quite clear I would have never written a book about it. What may not be so clear however is that had I never taken LSD, I strongly doubt I ever would have written any book. I simply never would have believed myself able to write over seventy thousand words on any topic. Now, even before having finished this book, I already have several others planned.

The Meaning of Life

"Now all my tales are based on the fundamental premise that common human laws and interests and emotions have no validity or significance in the vast cosmos-at-large.... To achieve the essence of real externality, whether of time or space or dimension, one must forget that such things as organic life, good and evil, love and hate, and all such local attributes of a negligible and temporary race called mankind, have any existence at all."

H.P. Lovecraft

It may seem rather presumptuous or bold of me to name a chapter "The Meaning of Life"; so let me first clarify that everything you read here is what I myself have learned, discovered or thought about, as it is relevant to me personally. I believe that it is quite likely also relevant to you, despite that I probably do not know you at all; but I could be wrong. I hope at the very least that reading these thoughts will give you some insight in to how the LSD experience has influenced my thoughts on the subject, and indeed vice-versa.

Before discussion of my thoughts surrounding the meaning of life, it is worth clarifying what I mean by the statement in general. I am using the phrase in the context of 'purpose'. As in: "What should I do with my life?"; "Why am I here?"; "What's it all for?"; and so on. Other interpretations of the phrase such as "How do you define life compared to non-life?" are certainly very interesting questions (both from the point of view of a linguist and a scientist), but they are not questions that are particularly relevant to this book.

In many ways, my opinion on the meaning of life helped to shape my LSD experiences, including the decision and desire to experience more of the LSD state of mind after my first time. However, in many other ways my opinions on the meaning of life have also been shaped by my psychedelic experiences.

I can not honestly say with any certainty which has had more of an effect on the other, only that they have mutually affected each other to significant degrees. As my decision to continue taking LSD after the first time was shaped by my thoughts on the subject and I had not yet taken it very often, it seems clear that my opinions and state of mind at the time were at least in some way 'right' for further experiences before having been shaped by the experiences themselves.

It is also of course true that the meaning of life to me is shaped significantly by my lack of belief in any kind of 'higher power' or 'afterlife'. I believe that you are born, you live, you die; and after you are gone, there is no 'you' anymore to experience anything[1]. As mentioned in the introduction to this book, if your beliefs are otherwise, we will have to agree to disagree. In that case, a significant amount of the remainder of this chapter is probably something you will disagree with, but you may at least find it interesting even if you think it is wrong.

This view of life is often called depressing; and it certainly can be if you do not think it through. Without a 'goal', such as reaching the right kind of afterlife, or pleasing some god or other, it really is quite easy to get trapped in thinking that it is all pointless and meaningless.

I myself was trapped in this way for quite some time and spent a large amount of my late childhood and teenage years quite depressed and despondent about it. In many ways life *is* meaningless from a grand perspective – the universe certainly does not 'care' how you live your life. Even if you were to become the person that ends up developing a super-weapon that blows up planet earth and all life on it (let's hope not), it really is barely a blip on the radar in comparison to the vast scales and energies going on in our universe on a daily basis.

But what I have come to learn is that this 'grand perspective' is not actually relevant for thoughts about the meaning of life –

---

[1] With the possible caveats described by my idea mentioned in the previous chapter, however as stated, I don't necessarily believe it to be true without having further evidence for the assumptions made.

we do not need to look at the grand perspective but only our own. In actuality, we measure our effect on our world and our world's effect on us on the limited scale of our immediate environment.

We do not concern ourselves in our day to day lives with whether or not other planets half-way across the galaxy are being destroyed by asteroid impacts, exploding stars or direct blasts of powerful radiation from nearby pulsars. Those things would be of great importance to us if they were happening *here* but not when they happen elsewhere. They are certainly things we study with scientific interest, but they do not affect us emotionally. We do not feel any pain or loss at the destruction of entire solar systems, and yet we do at the death of a single kitten or ruination of a single piece of art.

So, if the outside universe does not care about us and we do not (emotionally) care about it either, then we can narrow our field of importance for deciding the meaning of life. What matters to us, as people, is 'how we feel'. We care about the kitten and the piece of art – that means that we attach feelings to them. This 'feeling' therefore should form a kind of basis for any discussion of a personal 'meaning of life'.

An important aspect of 'how we feel' – for the vast majority of us – is other people. We are hardwired to care about things like our family and friends, even when it does not make obvious logical sense to do so. This is not the only aspect of course, but it is nevertheless a very important one.

To give a simple – and hopefully commonly shared – example: As a father, I can say that my daughter is the most important person in the world to me; but there is really no 'logical' reason for it from a cold objective perspective. She costs me significant time and money; she increases my stress levels; and she stops me having the freedom to do many things I would like to do if she were not in my life. But, it doesn't matter – she's my daughter. I love her with all my heart, and I wouldn't give her up for anything.

This is an effect of the way our brains are wired. The complex patterns of electrochemical reactions going on inside our heads define these thoughts and feelings. And it is not without good reason – if we did not have these kinds of familial attachments, we would never have survived as a species. Evolution brought us to do so because those cousins of our distant ancestors that did not form these attachments simply were not as successful as we were at spreading their genes.

Love and empathy – be they for a child, a sibling, a parent, a friend, a spouse, or whatever other familial or social relation – are good feelings. They can and do cause many problems at times, but they quite simply feel good, so we are happy to have them anyway.

To me, it therefore seems quite clear that the meaning of life is to have as many 'good feelings' as possible while reducing 'bad feelings' as much as possible. In the world of philosophy, this concept is referred to as 'hedonism'; but it is a word that I need to be careful with, as for people that have not studied philosophy (or at the very least, read a few Wikipedia articles), it often conjures up imagery that is not at all accurate for a real understanding of the concept.

This kind of hedonism is not about doing whatever makes you feel good with no regard for the consequences as is often assumed when the word 'hedonism' is used. That itself would not maximise the amount of good feelings in your life as there are many negative side effects to doing so that may make your life more miserable, or even cut it drastically short, reducing the *overall* amount of good feelings you can have. An extreme example is opiate addicts (e.g. heroin, morphine, opium, etc.) – opiates make you feel good... *very good*. It also happens that they'll also destroy your life if abused; and so while you may feel very good for a while when abusing opiates, your life will overall be significantly less happy than if you were to take a different approach.

Another example – all too common sadly – is selfish behaviour. The kind of hedonism I describe and ascribe to generally does not lead to destructive selfishness[1]. I may get an immediate gain from taking from others without giving back, but in the long run, I will lose out as others stop allowing me to take at all.

So instead, conscious effort needs to be expended to determine *"how do I maximise my good feelings?"* It is not an easy question to answer, and quite certainly something that no one is going to get one hundred percent right. However, it can be treated as a goal to work towards, even if it will never be reached. In the same way that science can be said to have the unreachable goal of 'describing everything in nature with perfect accuracy' with each new discovery or theory bringing us a little

---

[1] I make a distinction between 'selfishness' and 'destructive selfishness' due to the common argument that all behaviour is inherently selfish in that even without an obvious physical reward it is only done for the mental reward of 'feeling good about doing it'. This is called 'psychological egoism' and itself is an arguable topic, however for succinctness it's not worth discussing here.

closer; we can all individually work towards maximising our good feelings 'step-by-step' as it were with each new thing that we learn about ourselves and our individual worlds, even if we'll never hit that theoretical maximum.

Good feelings are more than just 'happiness'. Happiness itself is often – and in fact usually – a by-product of other good feelings rather than being the direct consequence of an action. Most good feelings are in fact things like pride, accomplishment, satiety, as well as the aforementioned love and empathy. Feeling these things makes you happy.

At least for me, one very powerful good feeling is the feeling I have when I learn something new – it's a little like pride and a little like accomplishment, but not exactly the same as either. I think this is common amongst people that gravitate to the sciences; as the sciences provide an avenue of constant learning – one in which no matter how much you learn, there is always more. It is a veritable all-you-can-eat buffet of opportunities for this feeling.

The sciences provide this avenue, but they are not the only thing that does. An LSD experience – as you have learned in the previous chapters – provides a way to learn about yourself and your environment in potentially unexpected new ways. Instead of knowing that you don't know something and then finding out, it is the much more powerful feeling of finding out something that you didn't even know you didn't know. It is a far greater feeling by far.

For this reason perhaps above all others, I continue to be attracted to the psychedelic experience. It provides the opportunity for constant discovery and betterment of myself;

even when I might otherwise naïvely believe there is nothing more I could possibly learn on the subject.

Beyond LSD and other psychedelics, there are other substances that lend themselves well to this 'hedonistic' approach towards life.

MDMA – as mentioned more than once in this book – is in a class of substances often referred to as 'empathogens' meaning *"creates empathy"* or 'entactogens', meaning *"creates feelings within"*[1]. Because of these properties, MDMA has some definite positive value in medicinal psychotherapeutic settings, as well as for those using it in a kind of self-psychotherapy.

I personally do not consider MDMA as widely useful as the psychedelics (and above all, LSD) because while it has some definite uses, they are neither as broad nor as deep as what LSD provides. That said however, I have found it very useful for strengthening bonds with close friends as well as simple enjoyment of my life and so I would feel terribly remiss if I did not mention it here when discussing the idea that 'maximising good feelings' is 'the meaning of life'.

On a recent LSD trip that I took – purely for the purpose of recording my thoughts to add to this book – I also had an experience that I believe has helped me better understand my own development as a person – the growth that happens mentally and emotionally as I take my journey through life; and

---

[1] Both directly comparable to the word 'entheogen' meaning "creates the divine within" as mentioned earlier.

additionally the importance and value of the relationship I have with my wife Lindsay.

On this particular trip, I had a period of time where I was simply lying quietly on my couch and allowing my mind to wander to anything and everything. So many images and thoughts passed through my mind that I could not possibly even begin to describe them all here. For a while, it was chaos, but from the chaos came a multitude of images – both static and moving – that gave me opportunities to reflect on aspects of my life.

Eventually in the wanderings of my mind, I came to a beautiful set of imagery of an idealised world. In the centre of my vision were Lindsay and I caring for our daughter, held between us as if we were protecting her from the world outside. My vision expanded backwards, as if zooming out of a picture, so that I could see more of the world. Encompassing this centre – somewhat like a circle composed of two halves – I saw us as older parents; and then, as the image steadily zoomed out more, encompassing that in the same way was us as old people with adult children and younger grandchildren. The imagery moved ever outwards and I found that encompassing the last layer was Lindsay and I as the traditional and stereotypical Christian view of 'angels' (complete with fluffy wings and harps). At each level or stage, the complete image formed a circle, with Lindsay as one half and me as the other, however still allowing for the previous image to be contained within.

Suddenly, all of the levels of this beautiful image collapsed in on themselves and appeared to crumble as the clear realisation came that in the physical realm we're not all encompassing new things on top of the old – we're the decaying mistakes of organic chemistry that exist 'just because we do'. This seemed horribly depressing for a short moment, but then I ended up feeling comfortable with the idea in general, although it still felt like I had lost something quite beautiful and special with this change in perception.

While I was writing about it immediately afterwards though, my mind turned back to the more beautiful, encompassing structures that I had seen before. I felt that we – as conscious beings – can, should and do ascribe to more than just the chemical chances that put us in to existence. We, as people, can learn to – if not physically – then at least emotionally and dare I say it 'spiritually', encompass our former selves and grow on top of that in to something new. The thoughts I had about the physical reality were still true, but they were less relevant once it was clear that we are – at least to ourselves, if not to external observers or the universe as a whole – more than just physical beings.

With Lindsay, it was an implicit given fact to me that she is the second half that completes the circle – I didn't even stop to consider the possibility of her not being there completing it with me. When I finally did question it in my mind, long after the trip had ended, I could not picture any way that I could have encompassed my former selves on my own without smothering them completely. This has helped me understand the importance and value of my marriage to me far more than any other single event in my life so far.

Another major thing that I have learned through my experiences with LSD is prioritisation of things in my life. That is to say, deciding what is truly important to me.

It is a common phrase to hear, "*on their death-bed, no-one ever wishes they'd spent more time at work*". This phrase struck a chord with me as being not only generally and fairly obviously true[1], but also woefully incomplete. Why focus only on work as something that you won't wish you had spent more time doing?

I thought about it a lot for quite a long time across many different LSD trips. I realised every action, event or thing in my life could be categorised in to the two simple categories of *"I wish I had spent more time doing this"* and *"I wish I hadn't spent so much time doing this"*. But I could not make a list of things – life is just too variable; there are too many different things. Instead, I resolved to keep this in my mind. Every time I do something new, I consider which category it falls in to and then prioritise it accordingly. I understand of course that sometimes for life to continue to go smoothly and let me do the things I will wish I had spent more time on, I sometimes need to do the things I will wish I had spent less time on – that's a normal part of life and I accept it. What I no longer accept however is to spend a moment longer than necessary doing something from the 'should have spent less time' category; and instead to make the conscious effort to spend all available time on things from the 'should have spent more time' category.

This is of course really just an elaboration of the hedonistic approach to the 'meaning of life' that I began this chapter with. It however extends the idea from only 'good feelings' to the idea of looking back at it from the future, so that things that generate truly good feelings when remembered gain a higher priority

---

[1] I can imagine some theoretical examples of jobs that would be a counterpoint to this, but for the vast majority of us, it is true. I love my job in general, but I still would not spend more time there than I have to.

than those that only generate good feelings at the time that they are being done.

I will not say I always succeed in this, but as long as I keep it in mind, I am often able to at least approximate this goal. Since doing this, my life has been far fuller, richer and more enjoyable that I ever could have imagined it to be before. It is the reason that I married and became a father – two of the greatest and most influential things in my life.

At the start of this chapter, I mentioned the fact that my world-view is of course shaped by my lack of a belief in any kind of supernatural phenomenon such as religious beliefs. It is probably only fair to therefore spend a little time on the meaning of life in relation to a more spiritual outlook as well.

While I can not speak personally of such an outlook, I have encountered – and had 'friendly' arguments with – many such people that can.

Generally speaking, the psychedelic experience lends itself more to a pantheistic approach to the universe than to the strict 'God or gods as strictly defined beings' approach. Pantheism is the approach that 'God' or 'the divine' is an aspect of the universe itself, and that all things that exist within the universe contain this essential 'essence' that when together as a whole, comprises the thing itself. There are of course degrees of this – as with any religious belief – from the belief that there is truly no difference between 'God' and 'The Universe' (which is really more or less just wrapping up atheism in mystical terminology) to the idea of a conscious 'God being' that has an essence spread throughout all things within the universe. Pantheists by definition however do not believe in a 'personal God'.

It is a natural human instinct to ascribe purpose, intent or desire in otherwise inanimate objects – how often have you said or heard, "*my car doesn't want to start*", "*the computer doesn't like me*" or similar? This kind of thing is called anthropomorphism or personification – the ascribing of human characteristics on things that are not human. It is more commonly done when the target is something that is not fully understood by the person saying it, such as with computers and cars; however can even be said by those who know full well the technical reason for the situation they are describing.

One well-known statement from the realm of physics is Albert Einstein's famous quote about quantum physics when he said, "*God does not play dice*". This is both an example of a pantheistic statement (Einstein also made it very clear he does not believe in a 'personal God') as well as personification by attributing his pantheistic God (the Universe) the property of being able to choose there to be randomness rather than stating (more blandly) "*there is no such thing as randomness in the universe*".

These kinds of personifications are much more readily done during a psychedelic experience. You may ascribe emotions to inanimate objects such as "*that house looks angry at me being here*" or "*that tree is very friendly*". For me, these kinds of personifications hold no special meaning, however if you are the kind of person who can believe in concepts such as spiritual essence or universal consciousness, you may feel that LSD allows you to better access these things.

Traditional monotheistic beliefs such as Christianity do not generally fit as well to the LSD experience but depending on the strength of the belief, the experience may certainly also 'affirm' aspects of that also. Touching or seeing God's spiritual force within you; the feeling of understanding the size and scale of God's grand plan for the universe; and similar such statements have been made by strongly Christian people that have undergone psychedelic experiences.

Generally of course, the more 'stringent' practitioners of the common monotheistic religions are unlikely to deliberately use a psychedelic substance; however, to the best of my knowledge, there isn't anything specifically stated in any of the holy books of the major religions that would strictly forbid doing so. The closest would be a statement in the Qur'an that rules against 'intoxicants' – this however could easily be interpreted to only refer to substances that actually dull the mind, a group of which psychedelics such as LSD are quite clearly not a part. There is even less to be said on the subject in the Christian Bible or the Jewish Tanakh which both only have general statements against 'drunkenness' which may or may not apply to some drugs depending on your interpretation.

States of Mind

"LSD was an incredible experience. Not that I'm recommending it for anybody else; but for me it kind of – it hammered home to me that reality was not a fixed thing. That the reality that we saw about us every day was one reality, and a valid one – but that there were others, different perspectives where different things have meaning that were just as valid. That had a profound effect on me."

Alan Moore

From reading the book thus far, you have hopefully come to the awareness that LSD's main effect is a drastically altered way of thinking, brought about by a drastically altered state of mind. This altered state of mind allows you to examine yourself and the world around you in new ways and learn a lot of things that you may not otherwise have come across in your normal day to day thoughts.

LSD's effect of a changed state of mind is mostly a temporary one; in that when the trip is over, you will again think about things with more-or-less the same kinds of thought patterns you had prior to the trip.

I use the phrase 'more-or-less' however as – as I said right at the very start of this book – a real trip will change who you are. The most dramatic changes are generally a conscious decision – however one that is made by very many people that have taken LSD in a self-reflective state of mind; however less obvious changes tend to happen whether you are consciously aware of them or not.

Those in the psychiatric profession or similar sometimes refer to these states of mind as neural matrices. Each neural matrix represents a particular mode or way of brain functioning that is distinct and different to other modes. It is measurably different in brain scans.

Before discussing chemically altered states of mind, it is worth paying a little attention to 'normal' states of mind. No matter who you are, you most likely have different mental states for different situations all of which are 'you', but all of which are different from one another. Importantly, each of these is truly a different neural matrix and is not simply aspects of the same 'normal' neural matrix taking dominance at any given time – you really are a different person in different circumstances from a brain activity point of view.

When you are at work, you think about work things. If you are in any kind of management position, you are required to be in charge and take responsibility for decisions. If you are not a manager, you are probably required to take direction from someone and do what they say – at least to some degree. In order to fit to these requirements, you put yourself in a specific state of mind and changing away from this state of mind may require deliberate effort.

I tend to watch people and pay attention to things like behaviour and personal interaction, as it is something I have been required to do throughout my life due to Asperger's Syndrome. I have noticed that co-workers who take a phone call from their spouses at work will speak to them differently than if they take the phone call while not at work. This is not simply a case of them being busy while working and so wanting to end the call more quickly – their entire aspect and mode of speech is different. If the call lasts longer, they will eventually switch to the mode of speech they would use when not at work. After the call ends, they then take a small amount of time to adjust their speech and behaviour back again. As far as I can tell, there is an unconscious internal struggle to change from the 'work' state of mind to the 'family' state of mind and then back again.

Each state of mind that you put yourself in regularly may also affect other states of mind. That is to say, regularly imposing a particular neural matrix can have long-term effects on other matrices as the matrix becomes more 'firmly fixed'. Examples of this abound, such as how a change in job can lead to a change in personality; or learning a new language (which imposes new ways of thinking about things and therefore new neural matrices) comes with associated personality changes.

Another different state of mind that most of us experience quite regularly is deep concentration on a single task that requires fast reaction time. Driving a vehicle at high speed; playing a high-intensity computer game; or some kinds of sports can all put you in to this state of mind. In this state, you pay less attention to outside influences, long-term memory retrieval is mostly shut off, and objects outside of the area of your field vision that requires your concentration are mentally blocked.

Generally, we refer to this state in daily life as being 'focused on a task'. Next time you find that you have been in this state of mind for whatever reason (due to the nature of the state itself you probably won't be consciously aware of it until it's over – or becoming aware of it will snap you out of it), think about how your mind was behaving and you'll likely agree that that state of mind is quite clearly different to how you are in other situations. Perhaps even to the point that if you analyse it honestly, it seems like a different person.

Many normal states of mind are deliberately imposed. The social order we surround ourselves with demands certain behaviour of us. It is inappropriate to arrive at a formal funeral smiling and wearing a death metal t-shirt and ripped jeans. So we change our outward appearance and force a particular outward demeanour on ourselves in order to fit the environment. This is often likened to wearing a mask that covers your true self. When you do this regularly however, it becomes more than just an outward show. Instead of just 'pretending' or 'faking' being a certain way, you begin to take on those aspects internally as well[1]. Simply put, for most people, it is the case that after regularly putting on the outward appearance, the internal begins to change with it.

The idea of these kinds of character masks is not a modern invention – aspects of the idea were discussed with regularity by ancient Greek and Roman philosophers. Karl Marx is well known for exploring this aspect in his writings against capitalism and added new elements to the idea that continue to be relevant in political theory today. Much of Marx's understanding of character masks was influenced by his studies of Greek philosophy, however much also came from Friedrich Engels with whom he co-authored the Communist Manifesto. Some years later, the Swiss psychologist Carl Jung developed a humanist approach to the theory – primarily using the term 'persona' – that is still referred to today in diverse fields of sociology, philosophy, and psychology.

Wearing these kinds of masks or personas is a normal part of human behaviour in any civilisation and should not be thought of as something negative as a general concept. Certainly, there are many negatives associated with masks, but it is doubtful that a modern civilisation could function very well (if at all) if everyone were to truly be their 'inner self' at all times and never hide themselves behind a mask. We grow up in a society that expects certain behaviours, and without some kind of massive

---

[1] Unfortunately, I can't speak of this first hand, as this is one of primary aspects of Asperger's Syndrome – I have to continue to fake it and 'play-act' my whole life.

worldwide revolution, the only way to succeed in society is to – at least occasionally – wear such a mask.

Just as with a physical mask however, these character masks have the primary purpose of hiding aspects of the self, whilst simultaneously presenting a false appearance. Simply keeping this in mind goes a long way towards understanding your own motivations and rationale for your behaviour as well as that of others.

Given that we accept LSD provokes a change in the state of mind during the trip itself – something that is really impossible to deny – it should be possible to compare it to other kinds of changes of mental state.

The first and most obvious comparison choice perhaps would be to other drugs.

Most – but not all – recreational drugs produce a changed mental state. Many prescription drugs also do, but for the majority this is usually considered an unwanted side effect rather than the main purpose of taking the drug.

The best-known and most commonly used recreational drug worldwide is alcohol[1]. Being drunk is definitely a changed state of mind. When you are drunk, one of the primary effects on your state of mind is that you care less about things. This has many facets of course, from helping you relax by making life's stresses

---

[1] Alcohol, despite how many laws are written, is a drug just as any other. It happens to be one of the most physically and socially dangerous recreational drugs as well, but that's a topic for another book.

seem less important to making consequences of actions less important thereby lowering your inhibitions.

After the intoxication of alcohol wears off, this effect is also generally gone and there is at least some chance that you will look back on your actions and regret some things you did. For people whose inhibitions cause serious difficulty in their lives, alcohol may be helpful in showing them that it is okay to be a little more relaxed about things; but for most of us, it offers almost no benefit at all and can often be extremely detrimental.

Probably the second most commonly used recreational drug in the world is marijuana. Marijuana's effects are difficult to describe briefly as it can be quite varied for different people and with different strains of the plant[1]. For example, the primary effects of THC for me personally are that I experience difficulty concentrating; the world outside of myself feels sluggish whereby my perception takes a moment to catch up with the sense of movement of myself, which in turn generates a feeling not dissimilar to sea-sickness; and then I usually want to sleep (possibly after throwing up). That is to say, I experience basically no positive feelings from marijuana whatsoever and consequently do not use it.

---

[1] Contrary to popular belief, tetrahydrocannabinol (THC) is not the only psychoactive substance in the marijuana plant; and other non-psychoactive substances in the plant may also modulate the effect to a degree; so plants with varying levels of THC vs. Cannabidiol for example along with other substances such as terpenes (such as myrcene) will produce substantially different kinds of 'stoned'.

For some other people however, they experience a kind of mild euphoria. Everything in the world feels good and right. The altered state of mind can at times also lead to some enhanced creativity – however for many, the 'laziness' that is induced often interferes with any more complex creative tasks.

In conjunction with other non-mental factors such as pain relief, increased appetite and so on, marijuana certainly may be a beneficial substance for some people in some situations and is indeed used medicinally in some parts of the world. Chronic use however can cause more permanent changes in a person's normal neural matrices leading to apathy and laziness even while not under the influence in some users.

The entactogen class of substances also deserves at least slightly more than a brief mention. The best known substance of this class has already been mentioned several times earlier in this book. 3,4-methylenedioxy-N-methylamphetamine, or more simply 'MDMA'. MDMA is often known by the street name of 'Ecstasy' however many pills are sold as 'Ecstasy' that contain either a mix of MDMA with other substances or entirely other substances with no MDMA at all.

MDMA has a lot of potential for psychotherapeutic use, as the primary effects are reduced anxiety, euphoria and increased empathy. This is of course also true for the right kind of person using it in the right kind of way outside of a mental health environment.

The first time I ever tried MDMA, I was shocked at my own ability to empathise with others 'naturally', given that as someone with Asperger's Syndrome, this is something that I normally have to fake in order to maintain social relationships with people.

My good friend Sebastian is a strong proponent of MDMA use and states that it has made him a far more accepting, outgoing, socially capable person than he ever was before it.

As he described it to me, "*Under the influence of MDMA you generally forget that you need a mask in public, you simply portray your most core self, and you trust that this will be acceptable to those around you regardless of circumstance (hopefully your sober self has made the judgment call correctly to take or not take this drug at an appropriate time).*

The sense of empathy is greatly increased, so you will often feel you can pre-empt any emotional trouble if a conversation is getting tense. You will also generally be more honest about your intentions and feelings with people, which can be a blessing or a curse just as easily.

Physical contact with others and displays of affection are also greatly enhanced, so for someone who is generally speaking very reserved this can be a very revelatory moment, or it could be slightly unnerving if that person believes strongly enough that if they were not under the influence they would never do that. I find that in those people, it's not that they would never want to do that, but rather that they would never normally feel safe enough to do that.

Assuming you do not simply get high and dance all evening (which plenty do), and you actually take some time to sit and speak with friends, you will often discover for yourself what really means anything to you, since topics will generally and quite naturally come back to these core beliefs and feelings.

You can learn a great deal about yourself and the people you speak with, and if you are observant enough, you will realise that these things remain true when you are sober it is just that you are more skilled at burying them behind more mundane goals and desires.

That is MDMA in a nutshell."

From my somewhat limited experience with MDMA, I can not disagree with Sebastian at all, which is why I simply quoted him verbose instead of paraphrasing. It is a very interesting substance indeed.

Compared to all of the above however – including MDMA – LSD is in a class of its own. The experience is much deeper and more profound than 'lowering inhibitions', 'causing euphoria' or even 'increasing empathy' and the myriad associated benefits that come from it.

Not that there is necessarily anything wrong with these things – they certainly can and do have extremely valid uses. But on an LSD trip, your mind is opened to yourself. You see yourself and the world 'raw and unfiltered'. It is not always pleasant, but it certainly can be. Once you accept the experience for what it is though, you do not always need it to be. Viewing yourself and the world in this way, you get a chance to re-evaluate yourself, your feelings, and your view of the world that you are in. And, unlike alcohol or some other substances, you will remember it with clarity afterwards and can use this for your own betterment if you choose to do so.

Beyond comparisons with other drugs, it is only fair to also discuss the comparison between the 'LSD state of mind' and states of mind that are not drug-induced.

Some religions – especially those from East and Southeast Asia – place a larger emphasis on state of mind than other religions. Buddhism is an example of such a religion where state of mind is very central to the beliefs, with one extreme example being the school of Zen Buddhism.

Zen Buddhism is often upheld in humour as impossible to understand with jokes such as, "*Q: How many Zen Buddhists does it take to change a light bulb? A: A tree in a golden forest*". The underlying principles of Zen are indeed quite difficult for people to understand when they are first introduced to it and the use of cryptic sayings and teachings that require deep thought to understand ('koans') are generally the inspiration for the types of jokes such as this.

Put simply however, Zen Buddhism's fundamental idea is 'suchness' or 'reality as it is'. It is difficult to do this concept any justice without more pages devoted to the topic than belong in this book; however to grossly oversimplify many things, meditation in Zen Buddhism (and some other schools of Buddhism) is used to bring the mind closer to an understanding of reality as it is.

To me, this sounds very similar to what LSD provides – the phrase 'reality as it is' directly compares to the description of LSD's effect of providing 'an unfiltered view of reality'. Not being a Zen Buddhist – or adherent to any other religious belief for that matter – I can not tell you that for sure. However, as will be discussed in a later chapter, it can be shown with a fairly high degree of confidence that the mystical experience on LSD is no 'less real' or 'less valuable' than mystical experiences that are spontaneous or religiously introduced. It is my opinion that had LSD somehow been available in Southeast Asia fifteen hundred years ago, Buddhism may have taken a very different path indeed.

Similar effects – but to a significantly lesser degree – are described by practitioners of many forms of martial arts, exercise routines, and body/mind control exercises such as yoga or t'ai chi ch'uan. For the more physically strenuous activities, it is likely that at least part of the effect is a chemical one, commonly called 'runner's high' where opioid receptors in the brain are being activated (not dissimilar to taking painkillers such as codeine, morphine or heroin). However, for the less strenuous activities this can be ruled out and the effect is likely generated by the development of a conscious ability to block certain neural pathways leading to a state of 'inner peace' or acceptance which itself is the first step towards seeing 'reality as it is' from the Zen Buddhist perspective.

An oft-repeated term that you hear when reading or talking about psychedelic experiences is **'consciousness expansion'**. This is a phrase that I try to avoid using too often, because it can invoke negative perceptions in people not familiar with psychedelics. They hear the phrase and think to themselves that it's all "*a bunch of new-age bullshit*" (to directly quote someone I spoke with no so long ago). It's not that the phrase is inaccurate, it's more that it has been used (and abused) so often for so many different things that the real meaning is difficult to decipher unless you already know what it is the person really means when they say it.

As it happens, many uses of the phrase are not entirely incorrect. They talk about breadth of thought; or about depth of thought; or even about "*getting in touch with your inner self*". While they are not wrong, these descriptions are missing the point by focusing too narrowly on the effects of consciousness expansion and not on what it *really is* in and of itself.

When talking about consciousness expansion in regard to psychedelics, the phrase very specifically means 'having more consciousness'.

This may also sound somewhat confusing or meaningless at first; however, it is easy to picture if you go the other way around. Have you ever been 'less conscious' than normal? Pretty much everyone has at one point or another, and for many of us it is a regular occurrence. When you first wake up in the morning and are a bit groggy before you've had your morning coffee; or when you are daydreaming and don't pay attention to the world around you; or when you 'switch off' in front of the TV in the evening after work; these are times that you're less conscious than normal. You are certainly not 'unconscious', but you're also not fully conscious.

When you take LSD or (most) other psychedelics, you experience a state that is even more conscious than your regular state; just as your regular state is more conscious than your groggy-just-woke-up-and-need-coffee state. This comes as a surprise to some people, as they assume – quite incorrectly – that their normal state of being was the most conscious they were capable of being.

Being less conscious tends to mean you are less alert, you notice less than normal, you think more slowly, and the topics that you think about are both shallower and in a narrower range than normal. Being more conscious – that is, experiencing consciousness expansion – is therefore quite logically the opposite. You are more alert, you notice more than normal, you think more quickly, and the topics that you think about are both deeper and wider ranging than normal.

You may right now be thinking about the effect of a good cup of coffee in the morning. When you are groggy and 'less conscious', the coffee helps. So, is caffeine a substance that expands consciousness?

Quite simply, no. Caffeine increases 'alertness', but alertness and consciousness are far from the same thing. If you are less alert than normal, a side effect is being less conscious than normal and indeed vice-versa. However, after increasing your alertness beyond a certain level, you will see no further increases in consciousness. That is, you reach a plateau of consciousness that can roughly be called your 'normal' state. You can continue to become more alert, but this will never further manifest as an expansion to consciousness.

I have said several times throughout this book that a real LSD trip changes you. That the 'you after the trip' is a different person to the 'you before the trip'. A large part of this is to do with the expanded consciousness that you experienced during the trip. It doesn't completely go away afterwards – your 'plateau of normal consciousness' is just a little higher than before.

I already mentioned the idea of a 'normal' level of consciousness that everyone has – you generally are at this level, or below. When you take a psychedelic substance, you are pushed far above this normal level. After the trip, if you have been able to appreciate the expansion during the trip and make use of it, your mind will be more accepting of entering higher states in general. Because of this, your baseline 'normal' level of consciousness is somewhat higher than it was before the trip. You notice more, you feel more, and you think more about abstract ideas and patterns than you did before.

I am honestly not sure if this effect is permanent or simply 'very long term'. What I am sure of is that it has its limits. I believe that after around twenty or so serious LSD trips, my normal level of consciousness never rose any higher. Possibly, there is a kind of next plateau, and after you have reached it, your baseline level of consciousness will not rise any higher through the further use of psychedelics. Perhaps this is simply a limitation of the brain itself, and indeed there is no further way to raise the plateau higher still; or perhaps there is, but we have yet to find it. For the moment, I am reasonably confident in saying that my normal state of being is now 'the most conscious it can be' – compared to before LSD when my normal state was 'less conscious than it could be'.

The LSD trip itself is always such an extremely high level that when under the effects and comparing myself in my 'tripping' state to even my new 'everyday' state (let alone my 'before LSD' state), it seems I am going through life half-asleep. But my new 'everyday' state looks on my 'before LSD' state in a similar way.

Expanded consciousness – in a nutshell – is the LSD state of mind, elements of which may remain ever after the trip has ended. Everything else discussed in this book about the effects of LSD – both directly and long-term – is more or less a clarification of aspects of this state.

Where do I get it and how do I take it?

"Back in the 1960s and early '70s I took plenty of LSD. A lot of people were doing that in Berkeley back then. And I found it to be a mind-opening experience. It was certainly much more important than any courses I ever took."

Kary Mullis

LSD is an illegal – or at the very least highly controlled – substance in every country that you are likely to be able to find this book or want to be (about the only places it is not illegal are places where the rule of law no longer truly exists).

This means of course that the act of acquiring LSD is likely to present you with some difficulties if you do not already have a source already lined up.

First and foremost: Did someone suggest that you read this book, or loan or give it to you? If so – they are almost certainly someone who can get it for you, and it's (probably) not illegal to ask.

If not however, you are going to have to try to get it on your own if you intend to try it.

If you have the idea that you could perhaps produce it yourself, you could always search on the internet for *"how to make LSD"* or even read the chapter later in this book about the chemistry of LSD and try to figure it out from there, but I can guarantee you that unless you're a chemist or at the very least a student of chemistry, you do not have the necessary equipment or skill to do it yourself – unlike many other illegal drugs it is *very difficult* to make correctly[1].

LSD is generally manufactured in small batches by people with sufficient knowledge of chemistry to do so.

---

[1] Technically, the process of producing LSD is relatively straightforward; however, it requires specialised equipment; great skill and care; and a knowledge of chemistry significantly beyond high-school level.

It is generally the most available in towns with large universities. This is both a by-product of students being open-minded and therefore more likely to use it, as well as the availability of the necessary lab equipment for manufacture to take place using university equipment (or equipment acquired from the university).

Typical 'street' drug dealers in most towns and cities are unlikely to have LSD. Aside from this, they are generally not the kind of people you would like to associate with. This is a general rule only of course – I have personally met such 'street' drug dealers who were quite friendly, safe, and had access to LSD. They are by far the exception rather than the rule though, and approaching any kind of street dealer can be an extremely dangerous proposition that I would not recommend.

Most drug dealers however, contrary to what you may have seen in movies or on television, do not hang around on street corners waiting for customers to turn up. They instead have a customer base that contacts them and then visits the dealer's home or a specially designated location to pick up their purchases. If you are going to have a dealer, this is the kind of dealer you want to have. Finding this kind of dealer however may not always be easy.

One way, if you suspect that LSD or other psychedelics may be used in your area would be to find the kind of place where you yourself would go if you took LSD. The previous chapters of this book should have given you some idea already. Once there, look around for people acting unusually – perhaps in a small group of two or three and doing things like admiring trees, staring off in to space, or laughing at apparently nothing at all. These people might be on LSD (or if not, they are almost certainly on *something*!). As said, it's (probably) not illegal to ask and they are almost certainly not law enforcement officers; so, just go ask!

Remember of course that the signs that someone is on LSD may be quite subtle unless they have taken a large dose – often on LSD there are very few outward signs at all. If you are approaching strangers and asking, perhaps the best 'giveaway' that they have taken at least something that would imply they may know where to get LSD would be enlarged pupils. Several different drugs have this effect, so it may not be LSD, but it is quite likely something in the psychedelic or entactogen classes, so these people may at least know where you can start looking if they can't help you themselves.

Approaching strangers at random may however not be something that you are comfortable with. I know that I myself would certainly not be comfortable at all doing so, however I mentioned it first in order to at least give you the chance to consider the idea without dismissing it out of hand.

Aside from the obvious benefits, there of course are also risks involved with having a more 'permanent' dealer, as should they be arrested or otherwise find themselves in trouble with the law, there is a risk that you become a target of suspicion through association.

Fortunately, there are other alternatives.

At the time of writing this book, there is a 'darknet' website called *"Silk Road"* that runs through the TOR network[1].

This site has been around for a few years now and in many ways can be thought of as the eBay™ for drugs and other illegal items and services. Purchases are completed using Bitcoins[2] as the currency and the seller will send your product to you in the post.

Other darknet websites also exist for similar purposes, however as I personally have not had any experience with them, I can not in good faith recommend anything other than Silk Road.

This is generally a very safe and reliable method of purchasing LSD (bearing in mind that as an odourless substance, and requiring very little space, it is unlikely to be detected in the post at all).

You will need a little technical savvy to get up and running, but it is worth it in the end. Some suggested searches online are *"TOR"*, *"Bitcoin"*, and of course *"Silk Road"*. The information you

---

[1] 'TOR' stands for "The Onion Router" and is a way to anonymise your online activity by routing your network traffic through multiple computers all connected to the same system. 'Darknet' websites are sites that are only accessible when connected to this kind of system – as in, they are not accessible at all when using the 'normal' internet.

[2] Bitcoins are an electronic currency system based on cryptographic principles. While not technically anonymous, they are for all intents and purposes anonymous when handled correctly.

find from those searches should be sufficient to get you up and running[1].

So now that you have an idea of how you might go about getting it; assuming you get something, how do you know that it really is LSD?

LSD itself is a salt. However, due to the extremely low amount required for a strong effect (significantly less than one milligram, as described earlier) it is almost never sold or seen in the direct salt form.

In the pure salt form, LSD can be somewhat determined as such by switching off the lights and shaking the container holding it – pure LSD salt will produce small flashes of light. Unless you are a medical doctor with a licence to work with LSD, a high-scale drug dealer, producing it yourself, or simply *extraordinarily* rich, the chances of you ever seeing even a very small vial of pure LSD salt is slim to none.

In any form, LSD is highly blue/white fluorescent under black (ultraviolet) light. For any of the forms described here with the exception of unopened capsules, access to a UV light will quickly determine if the substance you have at least might be LSD. Note that shining the black light on the LSD will begin to degrade it

----

[1] It is of course probably safer to perform these searches from a public computer or using the "safe browsing mode" that is supported by some popular web browsers in combination with an anonymous proxy or VPN (virtual private network) system, otherwise your intentions may be obvious to anyone looking through your search history or to targeted checks of your internet service provider's log files.

immediately; however, the degradation will not be significant at all for a quick check of a few seconds, so if you are unsure of the substance and have easy access to a black light, I would recommend doing so.

There are really only three forms that LSD is commonly distributed in and taken: Small squares of blotter paper, gelatine tabs, or liquid. If you are looking at a substance of some kind in a form other than these, you should have strong concerns that the substance you have in front of you is not LSD. Other forms are not unheard of however and so it may still be LSD, however your suspicions should be raised.

Small squares of blotter paper (a kind of cardboard) is the most common form you're likely to get, either as a new purchaser or casual user. They are generally referred to as 'tabs' ('tabs of acid' / 'tabs of LSD' / etc.) but may also be called 'blotter', 'hits' (also a generic term for a specific quantity of LSD, generally ranging from 30µg to 150µg) or sometimes – potentially confusingly – 'trips'.

Traditionally, actual blotter paper was used, but today it is more common for it to simply be a relatively absorbent cardboard. It is usually – however not always – decorated with patterns, sometimes on each individual tab and sometimes over a series of tabs to form a larger image. This is called 'blotter art' and many examples of it can be found online as well as in specific museums and for sale as artistic pieces (without the LSD infused on the paper of course!).

The strength of each tab is unfortunately very variable depending on the manufacturer. Essentially, the LSD salt was prepared in a solution (most commonly pure alcohol) and then carefully droppered on to the blotter paper, which absorbs the liquid and embeds the LSD salt in a layer on the top. Some manufacturing processes also involve soaking the blotter paper in a bath of the LSD solution; however, this tends to produce single sheets of blotter with different levels of LSD over it as well as possibly damaging the blotter art, and so is not commonly used by experienced manufacturers.

Hopefully, your supplier will have been able to tell you the approximate strength of each tab and you can make an informed decision based on the chapter 'Your First Trip' earlier in this book.

The average dose of a 'good' tab is around 100µg or a little over. Common in many places is 50µg. Often there is a regional bias, so even from different suppliers, you may find that if one lot of tabs you get are a particular strength, other tabs from the same area are more likely to be the same strength. Just to use an example from experience: most tabs sold in Sydney, Australia are generally around 100µg; whereas most tabs sold in northern Germany are around 50µg (although also well under half the price, so it's not something to complain about!)

I have also seen tabs with up to 300µg, although such things are exceedingly rare unless you know in advance specifically that you're getting such. If unsure, assume between 100µg and 115µg and then adjust accordingly for future trips based on your experience with the first time. Many sellers will overstate the strength of their product also, relying on a lack of knowledge in their customers; or in some cases simply because they themselves did not take appropriate measures in storage and the LSD on the blotter has degraded before it reaches you, the end customer. On the aforementioned Silk Road darknet website, an estimated fifty percent of sellers will report their tabs to be between ten and twenty percent stronger than they actually are according to reports of laboratory research performed by one diligent customer.

To take LSD in this form, simply put the tab or tabs in your mouth; chew them up until the cardboard mostly dissolves; then swallow it.

Normally, it should be almost flavourless with a very slight bitter background taste that is close to imperceptible. Unfortunately, some manufacturers use cheap ink on the blotter paper and this can have quite a strong and unpleasant taste. Be prepared for this.

It is a common myth that such foul tasting tabs are 'definitely not LSD'; assuming that because LSD is nearly flavourless, that any taste implies the tabs are not what is claimed. While this certainly could be the case in some instances (and chemical analysis shows to be occasionally true), it is more common than not that the foul taste is purely due to the ink on the blotter paper. Generally speaking, it does not make financial sense for sellers to use a different substance – when producing a psychedelic, LSD is actually one of the best value for money at the manufacturer's side once you've got the laboratory equipment set up and ready to go.

Another myth that is often used to counter the above myth (falsely) is that due to the small size of a tab of LSD, there are no other substances that could have a powerful psychoactive effect and still be embedded on the tab. There are in fact several other substances that would fit on to a square of blotter paper; however as described above, it makes little to no financial sense for the seller to put a different substance on the blotter. That said, it is not unheard of, and blotter paper has been found with psychedelic substances other than LSD embedded on it.

If you end up swallowing the tabs before they are fully dissolved in your mouth, you should not assume that it is not going to do anything or that the trip will be weaker. You will most certainly still get the full effect of the trip; it will just take a little longer to come on. By no means should you just assume it was wasted and then take more.

Small squares of gelatine are generally the second most common form; however, these have – in the author's experience – become somewhat less common over the last decade. They are occasionally also called 'tabs' as with the blotter paper, but the most common name is 'window panes' or simply 'panes'. The generic terms of 'hits' and 'trips' also get applied to this form as with blotter tabs.

Window panes are produced by mixing an LSD solution with gelatine. Often flavoured gelatine is used both for the colour and taste.

The typical strength of a window pane is significantly higher than tabs, due to there being more of the original solution in it. I have seen window panes vary from 80µg at the minimum, up to around 500µg. For this reason, it is important that you are aware in advance of the strength of it before taking it. If you are not sure, assume you are going to trip (prepare as normal), then try between a quarter and a half of the window pane based on what you have been told it is. It may do nothing, in which case the pane is probably around 100µg. It may also however be quite effective.

To take LSD in window pane form, simply put the window panes in your mouth and let them dissolve directly with your saliva. This will happen quite quickly. Once it is fully dissolved, you can swallow it. Some people claim that dissolving it under the tongue will cause the trip to come on more quickly, however there is no evidence for this nor is there any sound reasoning that it would be the case.

As with the tabs, swallowing it before it is fully dissolved will not nullify the LSD. Unlike tabs however, it also will not significantly delay the onset of the trip.

A variant of window panes is 'gel tabs'. This variant looks similar to window panes except that it bulges somewhat in the middle like a small gelatine sack containing a liquid. These are simply a different gelatine setting process to the standard window panes and contain approximately the same amount of LSD. They are taken in exactly the same way; however it is possible that they do in fact contain a liquid in the middle and so cutting them in halves or quarters is usually not an option.

You are less likely to get your LSD in liquid form unless you are getting it directly from a manufacturer (in major university towns, this is more common however as many manufacturers are students of chemistry with access to the necessary advanced laboratory equipment).

LSD as a clear liquid is simply the solution that I referred to above. It is usually sold so that one 'drop' from an eyedropper is around 100μg. The manufacturer however may have used a completely different dilution to this and there is no realistic way that you can test it without simply trying it. If you were not informed in advance regarding the strength, I advise simply trying one drop from an eyedropper and seeing how it goes. Be warned however that if you are unlucky, you may be in for a very strong trip. You most certainly should always try your best to be informed of the strength beforehand.

There are several ways you can take the LSD when you have it as a liquid. When I use the word 'drop', I mean one normal sized drop from an eyedropper.

One method for taking liquid LSD is to drop it in to a glass or bottle of drink. Note however that chlorine will break down LSD very quickly, so tap-water is not advised. Generally, I advise against this method unless you are sure that your drink will not chemically interfere with the LSD.

Another much more common method is to drop it on to a sugar cube and then let the sugar cube dissolve in your mouth. I can recommend this method as it is easy, has no unpleasant taste associated, and the LSD itself will remain relatively stable in the sugar cube if protected from light. In the past at places where LSD consumption was frequent such as certain kinds of concerts or 'love-ins', LSD could even be purchased directly in a sugar cube, usually wrapped in aluminium foil. I personally have never seen it sold directly in this form however and my research indicates that it is generally only extremely rarely sold in this form due to the smaller target audience today than there once was. At certain kinds of festivals or so on however, this form may occasionally still be found.

Dropping it on to a small square of folded tissue paper and then taking that as you would a tab is also a relatively common method for taking liquid LSD, however I personally fail to see the appeal of this over other methods.

And you could of course always just drop it directly on to your tongue. Doing this however, it is important to be careful – if you have an eyedropper with five drops in it, accidentally dropping it all in to your mouth at once is going to cause a much more powerful trip than you were prepared for!

If you have significant amounts of liquid, you could also of course produce your own tabs or window-panes and then take those. I advise against taking this option unless you are very aware of the strength of a drop beforehand and additionally are planning on distributing/selling it yourself relatively quickly. Storage of a liquid is generally simpler and more stable than storage of other forms.

If you have been sold something with the claim that it is LSD, but you have received some small solid pills; then firstly and foremost, if you bought these pills from some 'random dealer' rather than a trusted producer or friend, there is an extremely high chance the pills you have are not LSD. LSD is only *very* rarely sold in the form of a pill you would readily recognise as a 'normal looking' pill; however it is not totally unheard of.

One type of pill that far more likely to be LSD than 'normal looking pills' is called a 'microdot'. These called such because they are extremely small – generally only a quarter of a centimetre in diameter. The reason these can be considered 'almost certainly LSD' is that very few other substances could be contained in such a small pill (along with the binder to hold it together as a pill) and still have a powerful psychoactive effect – not that there are no other substances, but as mentioned earlier, it is usually not financially feasible for the manufacturer.

It is worth noting that a microdot could theoretically weigh up to around 7.5mg at this size and so could theoretically contain a very large amount of LSD. However in practice, almost all microdots commonly sold in the first decade of the 21st Century are between 40µg and 70µg. If unsure, assume 50µg and then adjust accordingly for future trips.

Often when people talk about 'pills' they really mean 'capsules' as with the kinds of capsules that many medicines come in. Capsules containing LSD are almost as rare as actual pills and so equally should make you immediately assume that the substance is not LSD unless you are somehow completely sure of the person who told you that it is, or are in some way able to test it yourself.

Generally speaking, capsules were used from time to time when LSD was still new and being used in mental health (quite successfully in some cases; and disastrously in others, but more on that in an upcoming chapter). Even during that time however, liquid was, and still is, far more common. Since that time, due to the other more simple methods, there is little incentive for a manufacturer to put their LSD in to this form.

Unless it is labelled, there is almost no way to determine the amount of LSD in a capsule – or if it is even LSD – without simply trying it. If you want to be cautious, carefully open one of the capsules and empty out the contents on to a clean white dish or a mirror. There are two possibilities for what you will find inside – powder or liquid.

If it is a powder, it should be almost entirely 'filler'. This is generally a white powdery inert substance (e.g. glucose powder, flour, fine grained sugar, or similar). A taste test should confirm the filler is indeed just filler. Any 'acrid' taste would be an indication that it is not filler and is in fact some other drug. Assuming it is filler, you can be somewhat more confident that the capsule also therefore contains LSD. Very close examination (a powerful magnifying glass or microscope on a low magnification setting) should reveal salt crystals in amongst the powder. This would be the LSD itself. Realistically speaking, there is no sensible way to judge the quantity of it – and therefore strength – without access to some rather specific laboratory measuring scales. If you had access to that kind of laboratory equipment, you could of course also then confirm with certainty that the salt found is indeed LSD.

If what you find inside the capsule is a liquid, it may be an LSD solution (possibly slightly thickened with a small amount of gelatine; however equally as likely not). In this case, as before there is no way to judge other than to take it without access to some rather specialised laboratory equipment. A taste test of the liquid could reveal it to be 'likely' LSD if it tastes either completely flavourless, or like alcohol; however at that point, you have now taken the unknown drug for better or worse...

Generally speaking, with any of the forms of LSD there is going to be a risk of taking an unknown dosage. This is something you need to be prepared for and caution is advised. Remember that if you take too little, you can always take more once you are sure the effects are not going to get any stronger; but if you take too much, there is not really anything you can do about it.

LSD Research and Medicine

"I don't know if you realize this, but there are some researchers – doctors – who are giving this kind of drug to volunteers, to see what the effects are, and they're doing it the proper scientific way, in clean white hospital rooms, away from trees and flowers and the wind, and they're surprised at how many of the experiments turn sour. They've never taken any sort of psychedelic themselves, needless to say. Their volunteers - they're called 'subjects,' of course - are given mescaline or LSD and they're all opened up to their surroundings, very sensitive to colour and light and other people's emotions, and what are they given to react to? Metal bed-frames and plaster walls, and an occasional white coat carrying a clipboard. Sterility. Most of them say afterward that they'll never do it again."

Alexander Shulgin – PIHKAL: A Chemical Love Story

Prior to LSD being declared illegal over the span of only a few years in almost all countries worldwide, it was actively researched in the medical field – quite naturally primarily in the realm of psychotherapy at first.

There were many different kinds of research performed; both to better understand the effects of the substance, and also as a direct use of LSD to attempt to cure – or at least aid with – some conditions. Some research tests had highly positive outcomes and some were quite negative. In later years, it became clear that the biggest influencing factor was the setting in which the research was performed. When the research was performed in a 'sterile' environment of white walls and metal bedframes, the test subjects generally reacted much more poorly than when it was performed in a comfortable and/or interesting environment.

Research dried up for a long time after LSD was made illegal. In more recent years, there has been some further research – much thanks to the efforts of groups such as MAPS – however on a much more limited scale due to the difficulties with legally manufacturing LSD and obtaining the necessary permissions to use it in human trials.

This chapter details some – but by no means all – representative cases of research that has been performed on or with LSD, hopefully giving you a better understanding of some of the effects it can have and the practical applications that these effects may have.

The initial ideas for medical use of LSD stem from the changes in perception that are experienced when under its influence. The obvious field of research that was therefore targeted was that of psychotherapy, where it continues to be researched to this day (generally in a significantly lower capacity due to the legal status causing difficulties for research in many places as mentioned).

Most initial research in psychotherapy focused on the idea of understanding delirium or psychoses. In the understanding of the researchers, the effects of LSD appeared to be modelling a mental disorder, and so the thought was that it would allow the researchers to better understand the state of mind of their patients suffering from mental illnesses. They thought that they possibly even may be able to experiment with different substances that counter the effects and therefore may also have a positive working on actual delirium or psychoses. In many ways, this research could be considered catastrophically unsuccessful, as while the state of mind of someone under LSD may superficially appear to be similar to a mental illness, it is in fact quite different.

Despite the failure of this line of research, it is rare that research is entirely unfruitful. Having studied the substance in great detail and realised it was not producing a 'model psychosis' they also came to realise that it had the potential to be used in actual treatment of some kinds of mental illnesses – especially those of a purely functional nature rather than those brought on by physical brain damage.

Research therefore then moved to the study of using LSD as an aid in psychotherapy for people with affective mental issues such as bipolar disorder, schizophrenia and so on.

In the late 1960s, Dr William McGlothlin noted that people involved in previous studies reported positive after effects on personality, interpersonal relationships and so on – even when the use of LSD was intended only to study the substance itself rather than have any therapeutic effect. Together with McGlothlin, the eminent researcher Dr Sidney Cohen performed a study focusing on this.

The results of the study showed that for the group taking 200µg of LSD, over 40% of individuals experienced 'some after effects' and just under 20% of individuals experienced 'deep after effects'. The most common effect was 'greater understanding' followed closely by 'greater introspection' with 'more tolerance', 'less materialistic' and 'less egocentric' all showing high values as well.

Clearly, this warranted a new kind of research – LSD as an aid for psychotherapy in 'normal people' as opposed to the mentally ill. The earlier chapter of this book, titled "Self-Discovery" can be thought of as detailing a kind of self-psychotherapy, where you act as your own therapist controlling the LSD experience for a positive outcome.

It was clear at this stage that the psychedelic experience offered access to a deeper, more 'raw' part of the mind than psychotherapy had ever previously been able to reach. Tapping in to this in the right way could potentially offer benefits of immeasurable value – changing months or years of therapy with only slight benefit to weeks or months with much higher levels of success.

The Czech psychiatrist Stanislav Grof has described it by saying, *"An important thing about psychedelic experiences is that they take you way beyond anywhere that psychoanalysis or some related schools can actually reach."*

Doctor Grof – as with many of the early researchers that tried LSD for themselves – became convinced of the powerful potential of the substance through having experienced it first-hand. Of his own first experience, he said, *"My first LSD experience was extremely powerful. It really completely changed my life professionally and also personally. ... By far the most interesting thing you can do when you're a psychiatrist is to study these non-ordinary states of consciousness."*

The results of the early research in to psychotherapy with LSD quite naturally lent itself to further study of the possibility of using it as an agent to help combat alcoholism and other forms of addiction.

At the beginning of the 1960s, many studies and trials were performed using LSD to combat alcoholism; with other substance abuse considered later. As LSD itself is a non-addictive substance, it was considered a potentially very useful tool for combatting addiction as it could be given without concern that one addiction may be replaced by another as is the case with many kinds of drug replacement therapies. In general, it worked much more effectively than most people would reasonably have hoped for.

Generally, a very high dose of LSD was used in these trials – between 400μg and 600μg in many trials with up to 1500μg reported in some cases. The intended idea of such a large dose was to induce a very deep experience, as disconnected from reality as possible, allowing the patient to have deep, profound, inner experiences – hopefully learning about themselves in the process and breaking away from their addiction.

In an early study performed by Doctors MacLean, MacDonald, Byrne and Hubbard, sixty-one alcoholics were given a high dose of LSD combined with traditional therapy based around discussion directing their thoughts to their problems. As opposed to an on-going therapeutic environment with multiple doses and therapeutic sessions over time, this trial was a single session only with appropriate interviews and analysis before and after the psychedelic experience itself. Thirty patients showed significant improvement, and a further sixteen showed some improvement. That is to say, over two thirds of the alcoholics benefitted from the experience, with around half benefitting greatly. Compared to the success rates of the likes of Alcoholics Anonymous or other support groups, this is an order of magnitude greater and achieved in an extremely shortened space of time.

As our understanding of psychotherapy for addiction has continued to improve, as well as our knowledge of psychedelic substances, it is clear that many things were not done as well as they could have been in these trials. The patients that did not respond as well may have benefitted from further experiences; and all patients may have benefitted more from a more comfortable and less analytical environment. I do not think it is unrealistic to expect that with our current understanding, yet better results could be had than were achieved in these early experimental trials.

In the 1960s, new research was also done in to studying whether or not LSD may provide pain relief in patients with serious or chronic pain. The pain itself was not relieved by LSD; however, the reduction in anxiety and distress caused by the pain was reduced, significantly improving the pain management from the perspective of the patients. These effects were noted even with sub-psychedelic quantities of LSD and patients reported lasting effects for up to a week after taking it.

While clearly not effective as a serious pain medication directly, this has led to further studies of using LSD and other psychedelics as anxiety relief in the terminally ill, combined with more traditional pain-killers to numb the actual pain itself if required. As anxiety relief, recent trials at John Hopkins in the United States have shown dramatic improvement in patients even after a single well organised and prepared treatment.

One realm of pain where LSD has been shown to be very effective is management of cluster headaches and migraines. This was somewhat unexpected and came to light only quite recently by comparison to other medical experimentation with LSD.

As of the writing of this book, migraine management with LSD is not well understood or necessarily known to be an effective management technique. I mention this first to underscore that if you suffer from migraines, you may find LSD a helpful treatment, or you may not – there simply is not enough research at present to say one way or the other.

Cluster headaches on the other hand are something different to migraines. They are often termed 'suicide headaches' due to the intense agony that they cause in sufferers that can lead to the sufferer either causing themselves significant physical harm to 'distract' from the pain of the headache, or in extreme cases, actually taking their own lives being unable to deal with that level of pain any more.

Cluster headaches often come in a somewhat regular pattern or cycle. Sufferers have made detailed diaries of their headaches, including what they eat, drink and do throughout the days, and use these to try to see if there is any cause for the headaches that they can determine.

In the late 1990s, a cluster headache sufferer that was keeping such a diary noted that he had not experienced a headache that year. Looking through his diary to try to determine a cause, there was nothing obvious as far as he could see. At some point, it dawned on him that the only difference was that he had used LSD twice during that year. Perhaps, he reasoned, the LSD had somehow interrupted the normal headache cycle. Intrigued and somewhat excited, he decided to experiment with other psychedelic substances and found that in general, they did indeed seem to help.

He posted his findings online, and was of course immediately met with extreme scepticism and doubt. Further investigation however, both by other sufferers and then later by medical researchers after statistically significant numbers of reports started to appear showed that there seemed to be at least a level of truth to the idea. Now, there is a large community of sufferers – even registered as a non-profit organisation in the United States ('Cluster Busters') that have further researched and developed these findings.

The Cluster Busters website primarily refers to the substances LSA (Lysergic Acid Amide) and psilocybin (magic mushrooms) for cluster headaches. They claim however that this is primarily due to the difficulty in obtaining LSD and the powerful (unwanted in terms of headache relief) psychoactive effects. Thus far, LSD seems to be the most useful 'recreational' drug for these types of headaches.

The other substances such as LSA and psilocybin do work however. This is due to a chemical similarity with LSD that will be discussed later in the chapter titled "The Chemistry".

Beyond the Cluster Busters, there is active research at Harvard University in conjunction with a private biopharmaceutical company (Entheogen Corp, in Boston, Massachusetts) in to the effectiveness of BOL-148, also called Bromo-LSD (a significantly less psychedelic form of LSD), that is showing extremely positive results.

When I spoke with Dr Torsten Passie from Entheogen Corp, he told me that he wasn't really expecting Bromo-LSD to be as effective as LSD itself – they simply wanted to conduct initial trials with a possible good fit that would be 'easier' to get the appropriate permission to work with. As it turns out, Bromo-LSD is even more effective than LSD itself; however it's worth noting that this doesn't mean LSD isn't extremely useful itself for those who need a solution to their headaches right now as it may be quite some time before this treatment is available to be prescribed by a doctor.

Perhaps the most surprising aspect with regard to cluster headaches is the preventative effect of LSD and derivatives. While taking LSD will most likely stop a cluster headache as it is starting to happen, using it a few times in a row – perhaps two to three times over the space of a couple of months – will have a preventative effect that can last from six months to six years. For sufferers of headaches that are used to taking strong pain medication with only limited effects and having no obvious method of prevention, this of course seems like a miracle – even if they have no interest at all in taking LSD for the psychedelic effects.

The research is still underway and there is a long way to go before we can expect to see a doctor prescribing LSD or a derivative for cluster headaches; however, initial results seem extremely positive and this is good news for anyone who has experienced this kind of pain.

As mentioned several times throughout this book, I have Asperger's syndrome, and I attribute many positive changes to my condition to my use of LSD. Objectively, I can not specifically say that LSD was truly the cause – many children diagnosed with Asperger's syndrome lose many of the symptoms as they grow to adulthood. Many others however do not.

There has been sadly little research in to the effects of LSD on Asperger's syndrome or other conditions on the autistic spectrum. One example of research that was performed was a study in 1966 on 'Modification of Autistic Behaviour with LSD-25' by Simmons et-al. Unfortunately, as with many studies in that decade, it suffered from many problems; such as only testing severely autistic people, and concentrating on children specifically rather than adults.

In my opinion, these two problems are relatively major ones. Firstly, severely autistic people are unable to benefit from discussion of their experience due to having little recognition of the outside world. Trapped in their own minds, they will experience the effects of LSD, but are unable to discuss it with the researcher beforehand in order to be prepared for the experience and afterwards in order to analyse the experience and gain potential benefits.

The other problem of course is that children – whether they have autism or not – are not mentally developed enough to handle the powerful psychoactive effects of LSD. They lack the discipline to appreciate what is happening and are likely to find the entire experience only one of being a dream – and quite possibly, a frightening nightmare.

There is of course also the ethical concern about dosing children – and especially children that by definition can not be made aware beforehand – with a powerful psychoactive such as LSD. In the time that this research was conducted, these kinds of ethical concerns were less considered by researchers, but it would be considered abhorrent by today's standard to perform such an experiment.

It seems likely that if LSD can be helpful for autism spectrum disorders, the research should instead concentrate on adults with less severe conditions on the autism spectrum. In this way, it could be guided correctly by a qualified psychoanalyst and the patients would have the ability to discuss with the researcher both beforehand to prepare themselves correctly and afterwards to discuss the experiences that they had.

Despite these serious problems, the research that was conducted did generate some interesting results. The children in the study interacted with the world around them far more than normal, even engaging the researchers in direct eye contact at times. There did not appear to be any concrete improvement after the effects of the LSD wore off, but I believe that this is likely due to the problems that I described.

Another avenue of medical use that has not been researched perhaps to the level it should is the use of LSD as a 'nootropic' drug in micro-dosages. Nootropic drugs can be considered 'performance enhancers for the mind' – the concept being a drug that makes you think more clearly, accurately, and quickly.

There is some evidence that LSD taken regularly (between once a day and once every three days) in doses too small to feel the effects – between 10μg and 20μg – has a positive effect on focus, creativity and emotional clarity. That is to say, the baseline level of consciousness discussed in an earlier chapter may also be expanded through micro-dosing without the need for a powerful psychedelic experience.

There is some active research in to this effect at present by Doctor James Fadiman, a well-known researcher who was quite active in LSD research in the 1960s, however there are yet to be published results.

In his book, "The Psychedelic explorer's guide – Safe, Therapeutic and Sacred Journeys", Dr Fadiman quoted Albert Hofmann, the discoverer of LSD, as saying that the study of micro-dosing is one of the most under-researched area of psychedelic research. I wish Dr Fadiman luck with his current research and look forward to further research in this area in the future.

Throughout the pages of this book, you may have found that in many ways, I talk about LSD as being a mystical experience, and about spirituality. Yet, in my introduction, I specifically mentioned that I am an atheist. This is no contradiction. Those with religious beliefs will often incorporate aspects of their beliefs in to the LSD trip – or may find their beliefs altered. Those with no religious beliefs however still experience that same feeling - the feeling that I personally describe as "*being one with the universe*". It is a sense of majesty and of complexity. It is a sense of the scale of things. And it is a sense of the wonder and beauty that is all around us. Whether you call it 'God' or something else is fairly irrelevant once you're experiencing it.

But, is it a genuine mystical experience? There are those who claim to have had – and we have no reason to doubt them – mystical experiences through their religion. Whether it be Zen Buddhists gaining control over their inner selves through meditation, or Christian saints having an experience of direct communication with their God; these are the 'genuine' mystical experiences. How do the mystical experiences of LSD and other psychedelic substances compare to these?

As it turns out – perhaps surprisingly to those that believe in higher powers – we can objectively say that it appears to be the exact same experience. A mystical experience that is had whilst on an LSD trip is no less of a mystical experience than one that spontaneously happened (whether you consider this to be generated by a 'divine being' or simply unusual behaviour of brain chemistry).

When I say this, the question of course must immediately arise in anyone with a scientific mind – how do you measure the quality of a mystical experience? How can you say that they are objectively the same?

One common aspect of mystical experiences is that they change a person. After a saint had been spoken to by God, they may have travelled off on a holy quest to fulfil God's will. Or after a divine revelation, a drug addict may change their ways and be clean and sober (this, incidentally is the intended effect of the religious indoctrination in programs such as Alcoholics Anonymous and Narcotics Anonymous; it rarely works however, as indoctrination does not in and of itself lead to mystical experiences).

We can objectively measure, using psychoanalytical tools such as precisely calibrated surveys like the 'Minnesota Multiphasic Personality Inventory', how much someone has changed from a previous measurement, or even how much someone is motivated or changed by a particular action or event in their lives. While the research is of course next to non-existent for people 'before' having a spontaneous mystical experience (without LSD use), it is possible to compare people 'after' such an experience with people who have used LSD and had a mystical experience; as well as both the 'before' and 'after' for people using LSD for the first time.

Blind studies where researchers compare the results of people who have had a mystical experience under the influence of LSD to those who have had a mystical experience spontaneously shows that it is not possible to tell the difference.

One specific experiment that is of interest on this topic used psilocybin rather than LSD; however, the effects are similar enough for it to warrant mentioning here. It is commonly called 'The Good Friday experiment' or the 'Marsh Chapel experiment' and took place on Good Friday in 1962. The experiment took place in a chapel, with twenty divinity students during mass. Ten students received a placebo, and ten students received 30mg of psilocybin.

There are many discussions about this experiment easily available online, and so I will not go in to detail or critique the methods used. The end result however was that despite some potential issues with the testing method and subsequent questionnaire, it was clearly apparent that the sense of the divine within the religious experience was greatly heightened by the use of the psychedelic substance.

Twenty-five years after the experiment – in 1991 – a follow up survey of the participants was conducted by the psychedelic researcher Dr Rick Doblin. The respondents claimed that it was from their perspective a truly mystical experience and one of the high-points of their spiritual lives. Doctor Doblin stated in his follow up paper that there is *"considerable doubt on the assertion that mystical experiences catalyzed by drugs are in any way inferior to non-drug mystical experiences in both their immediate content and long-term effects."*

This is of course highly analogous with the use of psychedelics throughout history in the religious practices of cultures beyond the western Christian culture. Commonly known examples include the ayahuasca brew amongst indigenous Amazonian cultures or the peyote cactus used in native North American religions. Even outside of the Americas, there is some evidence to suggest that prior to the Abrahamic religions of Judaism, Christianity, and Islam, the Indo-European cultures – most especially the pre-Hellenic Greeks and various Celtic and Germanic cultures – practiced rituals with psilocybin mushrooms. After the discovery of alcohol, it may also have been viewed initially as a type of entheogen. With the spread of alcohol, and then the Abrahamic religions, the use of psilocybin dwindled in religious use, however even by the time of early Christianity it appears it was not unknown and continued to be used in some religious rituals to an extent alongside cannabis.

Despite LSD being a relatively young substance – a newcomer to the stage of psychedelics – it finds itself a powerful new player in the field. LSD, subjectively speaking, produces much deeper and more powerful experiences than other psychedelic substances, and generally more consistently.

Because of this, it is of no surprise that governments with nefarious plans also had – and continue to have – a role to play in the research that has been done on this substance.

In the United States, a project by the name of 'MKUltra' was conducted by the Central Intelligence Agency in secret from 1953 to 1973, with some details eventually becoming known in

1977 and some further information being declassified in 2001. MKUltra was a broad project covering experimentation in to 'behavioural engineering'; or put more bluntly, mind control.

Many different techniques were investigated, including sexual abuse and other forms of torture, sensory deprivation, and of course psychedelic substances – most especially LSD.

The initial research in to LSD during the project was quite indiscriminate, with the target of determining whether the altered state of consciousness could be used to 'turn' enemy agents; or whether the enemy may be able to use it to turn their agents. It was administered to prisoners, mental patients, drug addicts, prostitutes, and men who visited brothels (brothels set up by the CIA specifically), under the theory that these people were the least able to fight back, or in the case of the men visiting brothels, would likely be too ashamed of their actions to talk about the experience.

Beyond the determination of whether LSD could be used to turn an agent to the other side, they also investigated whether it may be useful to 'wipe someone clean' and 'reprogram' them; and also whether it may be useful as a truth serum.

Despite a huge array of these experiments, including giving people LSD for extremely extended periods of time; dosing internal CIA staff without their consent or knowledge; and so on; the final decision was that LSD is too unpredictable and uncontrollable for these settings and uses. There was simply no way they were able to control the experiences to any significant degree other than to inspire terror in the individuals with no benefit to the interrogator.

MKUltra continued with other barbaric experiments, including injecting a barbiturate followed by amphetamine to prevent the subject from falling asleep. Whilst both horrid and fascinating to read about however, the focus of this book is on LSD and so should you be interested, I can only recommend reading more about the project elsewhere.

Beyond the use by the CIA, other government agencies in the United States (and elsewhere) also experimented with LSD. The United States Army conducted experiments to determine if LSD could be used as an aerosol weapon, rendering enemy combatants less organised and less able to fight. Eventually it was decided however that the chaotic nature of people under the influence of LSD may not always be beneficial from a military perspective in this environment, plus the risk of accidental self-exposure as with any aerosol based weapon.

The History of LSD

"*I believe that with the advent of acid, we discovered a new way to think, and it has to do with piecing together new thoughts in your mind. Why is it that people think it's so evil? What is it about it that scares people so deeply, even the guy that invented it, what is it? Because they're afraid that there's more to reality than they have confronted. That there are doors that they're afraid to go in, and they don't want us to go in there either, because if we go in we might learn something that they don't know. And that makes us a little out of their control.*"

Ken Kesey

So much has been written about the discovery of LSD that I feel it would almost be a waste of paper to expand on it too much here. In case you are not aware of the story however, in brief, it goes like this.

In 1938, a Swiss scientist by the name of Albert Hofmann was working at the Sandoz pharmaceutical company. He was performing a fairly straightforward task of producing derivatives of ergot alkaloids, looking for potentially medically useful substances. The name 'LSD' is simply an abbreviation of the German 'Lysergsäure-diethylamid' meaning 'Lysergic Acid Diethylamide'. It is also commonly known as 'LSD-25' as – quite mundanely – it was the 25th such ergot alkaloid derivative that he had produced during this task. The main intention of this particular derivative was to hopefully have produced a useful circulatory and respiratory stimulant.

Five years later, on the 16th of April 1943, he re-created the substance for further study. During this, he accidentally managed to dose himself with the substance. How exactly this occurred is usually described as absorption through the skin; however, subsequent tests as well as a better understanding of low-dose LSD effects have put this in to doubt.

Regardless of how it occurred, Dr Hofmann experienced some minor psychedelic effects for a short period of time. This piqued his curiosity, as it was quite unexpected. Many years later, when talking about the fortuity of this accidental discovery he said, "I didn't go looking for LSD, it came looking for me; it decided to ring my doorbell, to make its presence known... the world needs it now more than ever."

Three days later, on the 19th of April 1943, he deliberately ingested 250µg of LSD, expecting this to be a 'threshold dose' (the minimum amount required to have any kind of noticeable effect at all) based on the state of knowledge in to other mind altering drugs at the time. In reality, the threshold dose is somewhere around 20µg.

This relatively strong dose caused a fairly powerful psychedelic experience with pronounced visual effects and a heavily altered state of mind. Dr Hofmann asked an assistant to help him home and – due to restrictions during World War II – had to make the journey by bicycle. Because of this, this day is now often referred to as 'Bicycle Day' amongst LSD users and is considered the first true LSD trip (the minor effects three days earlier are not generally referred to as a trip).

With no idea what to expect as the trip grew stronger, Dr Hofmann experienced anxiety and fear. He believed he had somehow poisoned himself, and may have driven himself insane. It is important to remember that from his perspective, he had ingested only a small dose of the substance and was experiencing such powerful effects that to the logical mind of a serious research chemist in his late thirties, insanity seemed a reasonable deduction based on the symptoms at the time.

After arriving at home, he experienced feelings of dread that his neighbour was a witch with malevolent intentions towards him and that his modest apartment was a strange and alien place to him. Drinking milk in an attempt to reduce the effects of the 'poisoning' had no effect.

His doctor was called, but after he arrived, was unable to determine anything physically wrong with Dr Hofmann other than dilated pupils.

After a time, the fear and anxiety began to give way to more pleasant feelings and Dr Hofmann began to enjoy the trip in earnest. He reports at length about the visual effects he saw behind closed eyelids and with his eyes open as well as some of the thoughts that were going through his mind at the time.

The next day, he experienced the feeling of well-being, with brighter colours and the sense that everything was 'right' as I have described earlier in this book.

Fuller accounts of Dr Hofmann's experience are available from various sources; but I can not recommend anything better than to read the words as he wrote them himself in his book *"LSD: My Problem Child"*[1]. If I may say so, this book is a must-read for anyone interested in the history of LSD, or the effects that LSD has on the mind.

Dr Hofmann spent the rest of his life involved with LSD and other psychedelics. He is often quoted out of context, depending on which view the person giving the quote wishes to present – either that of the serious scientist, unhappy with his creation and against the use of LSD in any way outside the realm of psychiatric healthcare; or that of the happy-go-lucky trickster scientist, in love with his creation and surreptitiously practicing consciousness-expansion as often as possible.

I never had the fortune to meet Dr Hofmann, however in the course of my research for this book, I met people who had. Combined with the many quotes that one can find, I have formed

---

[1] Or, if you read German, the original version, published as *"LSD: Mein Sorgenkind"*.

a picture of Dr Hofmann as being somewhere between these two extremes. He seemed unhappy with the way LSD was used in some subcultures – with no reverence for its effects or care taken for the power of the substance; but also happy to have experienced psychedelic trips on many occasions himself. He seems to have seen a need for the psychedelic experience in the world – including beyond that of experiences controlled purely in a medical setting controlled entirely by doctors.

He perhaps said in best in the foreword to *"LSD: My Problem Child"*, where he wrote, *"Deliberate provocation of mystical experience, particularly by LSD and related hallucinogens, in contrast to spontaneous visionary experiences, entails dangers that must not be underestimated. Practitioners must take into account the peculiar effects of these substances, namely their ability to influence our consciousness, the innermost essence of our being. The history of LSD to date amply demonstrates the catastrophic consequences that can ensue when its profound effect is misjudged and the substance is mistaken for a pleasure drug. Special internal and external advance preparations are required; with them, an LSD experiment can become a meaningful experience. Wrong and inappropriate use has caused LSD to become my problem child."*

As detailed earlier, psychedelics have a powerful effect in combination with psychotherapy for those who need it from a traditional standpoint; but what psychedelics have shown me – and I believe Dr Hofmann would agree, if I may be so presumptuous – is that in a way, they can benefit anyone who is open to letting them do so when used responsibly and the right kind of setting. After all, couldn't we all benefit from a little psychotherapy in some way or other?

Of course, there is a lot more to the history of LSD than only the formal research. The counter-culture of late 1960s America is the best-known timeframe for the use of LSD outside of the laboratory; however, it has existed in some form or other from the discovery through to today.

If you read or hear the word 'Hippie' you probably have an image come to mind quite quickly. The image you have probably depends quite a lot on how old you are and on the culture in which you grew up. I myself was born after the hey-day of the hippies, and so my own experiences in my youth of hippie culture were strange old people wearing funny colourful loose fitting clothes and smelling of marijuana (not that I knew what it was at the time).

The hippie movement was not about LSD, but it embraced LSD as a substance that matched their attitudes, goals and beliefs. The subculture arose in the mid-1960s and shared some similarities – especially in language and counter-culture values – with the earlier beatnik subculture, but extended these values in the direction of peace, universal understanding and acceptance. They embraced sexual freedom; a strong message of peace, including very strong anti-war sentiments; and new styles of music such as psychedelic rock that inevitably sprang up from the flush of new ideas and thoughts.

LSD was an obvious fit to the hippies, both in timing and culture, as it provided avenues for consciousness expansion, giving the users a feeling of breaking away from the accepted cultural norms of the day.

While most of hippie culture was centred in the United States, there were similar movements worldwide including the 'housetruckers' of New Zealand, the 'New Age Travellers' of the United Kingdom and the 'Jipitecas' of Mexico.

In many ways, the hippie culture never truly ended, but instead many of the beliefs held by the hippies that were countercultural at the time have spread to become commonly accepted, if not at times 'normal' in modern western culture. Religious and cultural tolerance; a greater acceptance of eastern philosophy and beliefs; modern sexual freedom – including the almost standard acceptance of premarital sex as being both healthy and normal; and a greater consciousness of living in harmony with the planet by avoiding the destruction of the environment; can all be seen as changes that the hippie culture embraced and are significantly more prevalent now than they were prior to the hippie movement.

In the United States, where the hippie movement was most noticeable, it can be roughly divided in to 'east coast', centred on the northern east coast of the US; and 'west coast', centred primarily in California.

With regards to LSD, the two coasts developed somewhat differently, although ended up at roughly the same point.

On the east coast, most LSD use was initially that performed by serious scientists in serious settings trying to perform serious research. As is the case with LSD, many of these scientists found themselves changed after their own experiences with the substance. A small few began to share LSD and other psychedelic substances outside of the laboratory with friends that they believed may be able to provide further insight in to the substance. The author Aldous Huxley was introduced to psychedelics in this manner and described his experiences in some of his writings.

A common opinion amongst this fledgling East Coast culture was that of keeping LSD and other psychedelics for the elite thinkers – people who could truly appreciate, understand, and handle this kind of experience. Authors, artists, scientists, and others that used their minds either creatively or analytically should have it and everyone else should be excluded. It would help to improve them as people, whereas simply allowing it to be taken by anyone, anywhere would just lead to people using it improperly, dangerously and only 'for fun'.

Timothy Leary was a psychologist who conducted research with psychedelic drugs at Harvard University prior to them being made illegal. He was a strong proponent at the time of LSD's use in psychiatry. In August of 1960, he travelled to Mexico where he had his first ever psychedelic experience with psilocybin mushrooms as used in the religious rites of the Mazatec people. This eye-opening experience drastically altered the rest of his life, as he commented that he had learned more about his brain and its possibilities and more about psychology in the five hours after taking these mushrooms than he had in the preceding fifteen years of studying and performing research in psychology.

By 1962, Dr Leary's research had become so popular that the number of volunteers for psychedelic experiences had far outgrown the number of available places. Illegal distribution of LSD and other psychedelics outside of the research setting quickly appeared around Harvard University and Dr Leary was implicated in this distribution. In 1963, he was dismissed from his position with the university, ostensibly for failing to keep classroom appointments; however it seems clear that both his research attracting negative public attention from some areas and 'the wrong kind' of positive attention from others, likely had a significant amount to do with it.

Dr Leary quite quickly made the progression from respectable university researcher to counter-culture outlaw. He continued use of psychedelics and spoke publicly and loudly to all who would listen about the virtues of the expanded state of mind. Eventually, he set up an environment at his Millbrook Estate, where he introduced people to psychedelics and the psychedelic experience, and preached a non-religious 'gospel' of consciousness expansion.

In contrast to his peers who wanted to keep it locked away for certain people only, Dr Leary believed that anyone could benefit from LSD and other psychedelics as the experience itself, as well as other people who had had the experience, would help guide new users to the right path.

This fuelled and directed the hippie movement across the east coast of the United States. LSD was now outside of the lab and in the hands of the common man – for better or worse, it was there.

As a prolific speaker and writer, interesting quotes from Dr Leary are so diverse and numerous that picking just one to sum up his beliefs is very difficult. The closest to such an explanation is probably as he wrote in a book that he co-authored with Richard Alpert and Ralph Metzner called "*The Psychedelic Experience*", where they wrote, "*A psychedelic experience is a journey to new realms of consciousness. The scope and content of the experience is limitless, but its characteristic features are the transcendence of verbal concepts, of spacetime dimensions, and of the ego or identity. Such experiences of enlarged consciousness can occur in a variety of ways: sensory deprivation, yoga exercises, disciplined meditation, religious or aesthetic ecstasies, or spontaneously. Most recently they have become available to anyone through the ingestion of psychedelic drugs such as LSD, psilocybin, mescaline, DMT, etc. Of course, the drug does not produce the transcendent experience. It merely acts as a chemical key — it opens the mind, frees the nervous system of its ordinary patterns and structures."*

There is much more that can be said about Dr Timothy Leary, a man with a fascinating life who did so much to influence the culture and laws surrounding LSD. He was in many ways both a major positive force in spreading knowledge and acceptance of LSD amongst certain groups of people; and a major negative force for the exact same reasons, as other groups used his vocal outspoken nature to spread fear and mistrust amongst the population and ultimately demonise the substance far more than deserved. What we can take from this is that like LSD itself, Timothy Leary himself was simply a major force.

The progression of the hippie culture on the west coast took a different direction. Research there was more limited – although not unheard of, especially in and around Stanford university – and the existing culture of warm and sunny California was already more relaxed, open and accepting than that of the colder north-east.

How exactly LSD was first introduced on the west coast is not really known. What is known is that it started as a kind of an underground secret in the late 1950s or early 1960s. A group of people – most likely called beatniks by their contemporaries – that would later become the first true west coast hippies would introduce their closest friends to it in confidence as new and miraculous substance that would make you *"feel so much more of everything"* and *"really put you in touch with the universe"*.

This quiet culture grew slowly, and may eventually have led to a different kind of hippie than what did happen if not for an outside influence. This influence was MKUltra. As explained previously, a part of this CIA run project was to study the effects of different kinds of drugs on people for a variety of covert purposes. Some of these studies were done at several west coast hospitals, medical institutions and so on.

One research 'guinea pig' was Ken Kesey. Mr Kesey was working as a night aide at the Menlo Park Veterans' Hospital (mostly responsible for caring for mentally ill veterans); when he was given the option to voluntary take part in the experiments.

He was given a variety of psychoactive drugs, including LSD, psilocybin, DMT and mescaline. He kept detailed notes of the effects of these substances and having some interest in the beatnik culture – having written, but not published, a book about beatniks – naturally let his mind wander to make the connection between the experiences and some aspects of the beatnik culture.

This connection was furthered still as he spoke with patients of the hospital – sometimes whilst under the influence of psychedelics – and came to the conclusion that they were not 'insane', but rather simply had a different view of the world – and according behaviour – than what was considered normal by the rest of society. Not much later, his first published work, "*One Flew Over the Cuckoo's Nest*" contained many elements taken from his time at the veterans' hospital as well as ideas that were born under the influence of psychedelics.

In his words, "*too young to be a beatnik and too old to be a hippie*", and with a reasonable amount of money continuing to come in from the success of his book, Mr Kesey quickly became famous for throwing parties at which the drinks were spiked with psychedelic substances. He formed a group of friends that whilst always close, were somewhat transient, with people coming in and out of the group at a rate that it seems no-one could really judge or measure at the time.

In 1964, to launch his second published book, "*Sometimes a Great Notion*", Mr Kesey needed to get to New York. Instead of taking more traditional means of transportation, he instead decided with a group of his close friends, to take a road trip in an old school bus that they then painted in psychedelic fashion and named "Further". This group of people – which also changed on the course of the journey – were known as the "Merry Pranksters".

The journey to New York took the Merry Pranksters through a series of many adventures, containing too many things to be written here, lest this chapter exceed the length of the rest of the book. Suffice it to say, it was an LSD fuelled trip of epic proportions: sex with anyone who took a mutual fancy; dancing in fields; a stark naked woman standing on the back of the bus for vehicles behind to admire; and much much more.

Upon reaching the east coast, they decided it might be interesting for the 'west coast acid heads' to meet the 'east coast acid heads' and paid a visit to Dr Timothy Leary's Millbrook estate. They arrived as they travelled – loud and raucous. They were even letting off smoke bombs. At the estate, they were told that Dr Leary was on a three-day trip and did not want to be disturbed. The Pranksters found the residents at Millbrook to be altogether too sombre and serious; while the Millbrook residents found the Pranksters to be chaotic hooligans with no respect for the substance they were using.

After returning to California, Kesey and the Pranksters set up the 'Acid Tests'. These were parties with strobe lights, fluorescent paint, new styles of music and of course, a lot of LSD.

At the Acid Test parties, a band formerly known as "*The Warlocks*" performed for the first time under the new band name – "*The Grateful Dead*".

The Grateful Dead are arguably one of the most well-known bands of the psychedelic hippie era. Their music continued to be played live by some former members of the band through to 2009, with dedicated cover bands continuing to this day.

Fans of The Grateful Dead are often referred to as 'Deadheads' and as a group of people not directly related to LSD, have the highest consumption of LSD per person compared to any other group.

Despite the differences between the origins of the west coast and east coast hippie movements and especially the extremely negative view that the Pranksters had of the Millbrook estate residents and vice-versa; slowly aspects of both cultures began to seep in to each other. By the late 1960s, it would have been difficult to tell the two groups apart. There were people on the east coast that were more chaotic, and people on the west coast that were more introspective. There were people everywhere that learned to enjoy both aspects of the experience.

In 1967, the 'Summer of Love' happened in the Haight Ashbury suburb of San Francisco. The idea was to bring together all like-minded people to create a melting pot of every kind of thought. Different people from all over the US and the world came together and experienced music, drugs, creativity, and a freer sexual and social situation. It was inspired and started by the 'Human Be-In' event in January '67, where Dr Timothy Leary spoke his famous phrase *"tune in, turn on, drop out"*.

The media attention outside of the community was overwhelmingly negative. Residents of the suburb that were not a part of this new subculture found their neighbourhood overrun with long-haired young people listening to strange music and possibly taking drugs!

The guitarist from The Grateful Dead – Bob Weir – commented on the Summer of Love saying, *"Haight Ashbury was a ghetto of bohemians who wanted to do anything – and we did but I don't think it has happened since. Yes there was LSD. But Haight Ashbury was not about drugs. It was about exploration, finding new ways of expression, being aware of one's existence."*

After the Summer ended, people went home. But when they did, they took the experience with them. They returned to all corners of the US – and for some to their home countries half way around the world – and began to spread the word about this alternative way of being. It is fair to say that they had an indelible, if not always so directly noticeable, influence on world culture.

Two years later in 1969, back on the east coast of the US, the most well-known hippie festival of all time took place. Woodstock.

The Woodstock festival had thirty-two acts, over three days, for half a million festival attendees, when only two hundred thousand were expected. The weather was unpleasant with significant rain at times, which made the ground muddy given that the festival itself was held on farmland. Traffic jams made arriving on time extremely difficult for many visitors.

Despite the weather, the mud, the traffic, and the extreme overcrowding at the venue, Woodstock is remembered as an important event in history for the hippie movement, for rock and roll, and for the festival culture in general.

LSD was widely available at Woodstock and likely contributed to the relatively peaceful environment despite the many problems with the venue and weather. One attendee reported surveying the crowd himself to determine who was *not* 'on acid' at the time; he reports being unable to find anyone in his vicinity.

As the hippie movement began to fade away, public exposure of LSD declined as well. It remained on all lists of 'bad drugs' that schoolchildren are taught to keep away from (naturally with little to no explanation of the substance or any other), but in many ways slowly began to be forgotten by mainstream society.

By the mid-1980s, LSD was often thought of by mainstream society as something that 'used to be used, but not really anymore' and that attitude continues to this day to some extent.

Reliable statistics on LSD use are relatively difficult to find on a worldwide scale. In the United States at least, anonymous self-reporting is the most common method used to determine usage and as such, the reported figures are considered to be significantly lower than reality. Reported first time usage in the US increased slowly until 1980, decreased again until around 1990, began a slow increase and then sharply dropped in 2000 with a slow but steady rise since.

The main reason for the sharp decline in 2000 appears to be a successful raid on illegal LSD production by the United States Drug Enforcement Administration (DEA). They raided a production environment that was producing a reported one kilogram of LSD – that is to say, around 10 million standard doses of LSD – every five weeks. This likely accounted for around 90% of the LSD supply in North America.

It is however also important to note that the reported usage that is recorded is for *first time use* and says nothing of whether someone tried it only once, or if they continued to take it for a long period afterwards. Nor does it give any indication as to the setting in which it was used – whether for example as a 'party drug' or as something more, as described in this book.

LSD has never been an extremely popular party drug, however from the 1980s onwards, it gained a reputation as such in certain subcultures.

In 2013, the dance club scene magazine 'Mixmag' in conjunction with the independent specialist organisation 'Global Drug Survey' published a survey of drug use amongst dance club frequenters – the largest such survey of its type ever performed with over fifteen thousand respondents. Thirty-nine percent of respondents had tried LSD at some time in their life, and yet only eleven percent had tried it at some time in the last twelve months. Given the most common age of the respondents was twenty-one years old, it is reasonable to assume that of the eleven percent that had tried it at some time in the last twelve months that it was their first and possibly last time. It seems likely from these statistics that despite the reputation LSD has as a 'party drug' in some circles, the reality is that many users will try it, decide against it for that environment and then not try it again.

LSD use amongst people outside of the dance club scene shows a very different picture. An informal survey performed on a darknet drug discussion forum asking specifically for LSD use outside of the club scene provided just under five hundred and fifty respondents. Of those, three hundred and sixty one reported having used LSD more than once; and two hundred and seventy six of those reported using it on a regular basis of at least once every year. As all responses were of course completely anonymous, it is possible that some respondents falsified their answers, however as there is little to gain from them doing so, we can assume a reasonable level of confidence in the results obtained.

The respondents had an average age of thirty-four years, ranging from the youngest at fourteen years old to the oldest at seventy-four with a relatively even spread throughout, however a peak in the late twenties and early thirties. Ninety-four percent were gainfully employed, with technical professions making up a larger percentage than in the mainstream population; however as the survey was conducted on a darknet, this may be an environmental bias of the survey. Just over sixty percent of the respondents were male. The location of the respondents was not reported.

Of the respondents that claimed regular use, all but three – that is to say, two hundred and seventy three people – cited self-discovery or similar wording in their reasons for using it. The remaining three were all under the age of twenty and cited 'fun' as the only reason for use. Interestingly, although around sixty percent of the respondents to the survey were male, only around fifty percent of the regular users were male, perhaps showing a bias towards self-discovery in females more than males. The average age of the regular users was thirty-eight.

.

LSD and the Law

"Psychedelic drugs have been shown to cause paranoia, confusion, and total loss of reality - in people who have never taken them."

Attributed to Timothy Leary

LSD is a highly controlled substance in almost every country on Earth. That is to say, it is pretty much illegal to produce, own or distribute; with only some extremely rare exceptions in a very few countries where it is possible – by jumping through enough hoops and filling out enough paperwork – to obtain for medical testing purposes.

Of course, it was not always so. Before 1938, LSD simply did not exist at all; and before 1943, no one had the slightest inkling of the effects it can have.

For over twenty years after the discovery of LSD, it was not classified as an illegal or controlled substance anywhere in the world. During this time, it was investigated for medical use – often with many positive successes – as described earlier in this book.

In the 1960s, as LSD began to be used more and more as a 'recreational drug', began to be produced in underground 'backroom' laboratories, and came more in to the attention and view of the general public; pressure started to be placed on lawmakers by various other governmental groups and organisations to ban the substance.

In October of 1966, LSD was made illegal in California and not long after, throughout the rest of the United States.

In 1970, when the United States implemented their drug scheduling system in the form of the 'Controlled Substances Act', LSD was placed as a 'Schedule 1' substance. The wording of this schedule states that the drug has a *"high potential for abuse"* and has no *"currently accepted medical use in treatment"*. The statement made from the United States DEA (Drug Enforcement Agency) to support the scheduling was, *"Although initial observations on the benefits of LSD were highly optimistic, empirical data developed subsequently proved less promising ... Its use in scientific research has been extensive and its use has been widespread. Although the study of LSD and other hallucinogens increased the awareness of how chemicals could affect the mind, its use in psychotherapy largely has been debunked. It produces aphrodisiac effects, does not increase creativity, has no lasting positive effect in treating alcoholics or criminals, does not produce a 'model psychosis', and does not generate immediate personality change. However, drug studies have confirmed that the powerful hallucinogenic effects of this drug can produce profound adverse reactions, such as acute panic reactions, psychotic crises, and 'flashbacks', especially in users ill-equipped to deal with such trauma."*

As can clearly be seen from the research outlined earlier in this book, many of the points made by the DEA in this statement are simply untrue and the two main points to classify it as a Schedule 1 substance are both completely and utterly false.

The rest of the world soon followed the United States' lead, and by the late 1960s, LSD was illegal almost everywhere worldwide.

There are many theories regarding the core reasons for this rather harsh blanket ban on LSD – after all, on the face of it, banning a substance with so little potential for abuse or harm seems rather strange.

A common theory regarding the ban is the idea that the governments do not want to have citizenry that have experienced consciousness expansion, as it makes them harder to control. This is possibly a theory that actually has some merit, despite the 'big-brother' conspiracy theorist overtones that it conjures up. It is well known that the US government – in the form of the CIA and the military at the very least – were well aware of LSD's potential as a mind-altering substance, and the culture of the time was one of extreme paranoia about control due to the cold war. This paranoid desire for keeping things under control would naturally manifest as a fear of a citizenry that could rapidly undergo a dramatic shift of desires and expectations and so avoiding this by banning the substance that facilitates such a shift would be seen as a logical step.

Another common theory is that the US government wanted to control the drug trade themselves in order to produce money for covert operations; and so making substances illegal and cracking down on production performed by non-government entities would ultimately allow them to get a larger share of the money being spent. This theory may hold some value, but given the non-addictive properties of LSD and relatively cheap price in comparison to other substances, LSD does not seem like a potentially lucrative market. While this theory may therefore have an element of truth to it, there is little direct evidence, and if it were really so, then LSD would almost certainly have simply been caught up in the plan as a popular substance of use at the time and not specifically considered as a major interest over any other recreational substance.

Personally, I believe the most likely theory however is simply the idea that for most of the lawmakers in the various governments of the world, the idea was simply trying to look out for people as they may accidentally harm themselves while under the influence. This of course would be a case of gross incompetence on the part of the governments that simply didn't understand that LSD is – on the balance of things – significantly safer than most other substances used recreationally (including alcohol) by quite a large degree. Simply put though, I subscribe to the simple idea that one should never attribute to malice that which can adequately be explained by stupidity[1].

Of course, the idea that LSD presents a great risk and potential for harm had to come from somewhere. While most of the people involved in putting the law in to practice are probably innocent of malice (even if somewhat easily led – but that's not an uncommon trait in politicians), some group of people within at least the government that started the trend (i.e. the United States) must still have been responsible for the creation of the idea to begin with. Due to the anti-war movement that the hippies were strongly associated with, it seems fairly likely that the initial anti-LSD propaganda was primarily one of attempting to control a movement that was strongly against the current military policies of the government at the time. This of course also ties in with the already mentioned paranoia about control that was a part of the culture of the time.

Continuing legalisation against LSD seems to simply be a case of it being easier to maintain the status quo than to change things, combined with a general lack of any realisation that things could or should be changed for the better. This is especially true in light of the 'war on drugs'. The war on drugs primarily targets substances of significant more harm, but can not help catching less harmful substances in the same net. This is due to the way in which the associated anti-drug propaganda makes sweeping statements about all substances in general and

---

[1] Commonly referred to as 'Hanlon's razor'

the public (including politicians responsible for making laws) remain uneducated about the differences.

As it happens, there are in fact some exceptions to the laws for psychedelic substances in some countries based on religious grounds. As mentioned somewhat earlier in this book, another name for psychedelic substances is 'entheogen', which can be interpreted as 'creates God within' or 'creates the divine within' depending on how you wish to translate it. Entheogens have been used in religious ceremonies for millennia and continue to be used in some cultures to this very day. In countries of both North and South America – including the United States of America – specific laws exist allowing the use of certain entheogens in the religious rites and practices of native populations as well as (much more rarely) more modern or newly created religions. While LSD has been used as an entheogen in at least one small, not particularly well known religious group, no such exception exists or has existed anywhere for LSD.

Immediately after LSD was made illegal, research ground to an almost standstill. Shortly before the ban, Sandoz had stopped all exports to the United States by request of the United States government and researchers there were unable to acquire more LSD to continue their tests. In some countries in Europe, medical research continued to a degree, but significantly less than it had before.

Despite the ban, a few researchers were not ready to just 'give up' on what they saw as an extremely promising line of research. The researchers most familiar with the substance through personal experience most especially realised the great potential it has for helping people – and in ways that many had never previously even conceived of.

Some of these few researchers began conducting further experiments in secret – making use of LSD and other psychedelics in direct violation of the law. This continues to this day; however to a lesser extent over the years, and with the focus shifted more towards the use of LSD in mental health than purely study of the psychedelic experience directly. Psychedelic therapy sessions using LSD continue to happen all over the world in treatment of anxiety, alcoholism, and issues involving extreme self-doubt or social integration problems; just to name a few aspects.

The medical professionals using LSD in this manner are in violation of the law and would face extremely harsh penalties – including long-term jail and suspension of medical licences – should they be caught. Beyond that, their medical malpractice insurance will not cover them for this work; generally, no colleagues can take over their patients when they are unwell or otherwise unavailable; and they essentially have no support structure of any kind. So why do they do it? What do they have to gain?

Quite simply: they are medical professionals first and foremost. Patient care is the single most important factor and so to them, the most effective treatment for helping their patients is the one that they choose to use. LSD assisted therapy quite simply *is* the most effective treatment known to date in many of the cases that they deal with.

Beyond the researchers and therapists using LSD illegally, it is still possible in some places to perform legal research. Depending on where however, the legal avenue is often plagued with even more difficulties than the illegal.

In an attempt to reduce fraud in the pharmaceutical industry unrelated to psychedelic substances, many regulations now exist for dealing with experimental substances. These regulations help to avoid issues that plagued the industry such as researchers not publishing results that do not match a pre-determined agenda; faking dosages; and so on. However, these regulations also mean that research in to experimental substances is now far more expensive than it used to be. It would not be considered unusual for a planned experiment with LSD to cost in the region of one and a half million euro, where once the same experiment may have only been around ten thousand euro, purely because of the necessity to maintain compliance to these regulations with additional checks, paperwork and so on.

For large pharmaceutical companies testing out a brand new substance that they have developed, these costs are still a low barrier to entry – if their drug is useful, they will patent it and make their money back many times over. LSD of course was patented once, but those patents expired in 1963. So now – legal concerns aside – there would be nothing stopping anyone producing it, using it and selling it after one person or group had paid the costs that would allow research to proceed. Therefore, anyone planning to conduct experiments with LSD has no obvious way to recover these costs.

There are many different opinions on the question of what should be done about the legal status of LSD in the future. Generally speaking, these range from 'keep the status quo where it is illegal' through to 'completely legalise it and allow it to be bought at the corner store'. Most opinions from educated people who have seriously considered the topic are somewhere between these two extremes.

Given the non-toxic and non-addictive nature of the substance and the many problems caused by the current status; it is difficult to sensibly argue for keeping the status quo. On the other hand, freely and widely available LSD could easily lead to serious problems as people who are unaware of the powerful effects of the substance find themselves unprepared for the experience and end up in dangerous or potentially harmful situations.

The main reason that the status quo remains seems to be a lack of education, a lack of willingness to change on behalf of the lawmakers, and simple general acceptance from the public – most people simply do not really mind that LSD is illegal, as it is something they have never even stopped to think about.

That is not to say that some people haven't tried to educate the lawmakers. In 2007, Dr David Nutt – at the time, working on an advisory council to the government of the United Kingdom – and colleagues produced a proposal for a health policy paper titled "Development of a rational scale to assess the harm of drugs of potential misuse". In 2010, Dr Nutt performed the research based on this idea – the results of which, he published as "Drug harms in the UK, a multicriteria decision analysis".

In this research, a selection of different drugs were assessed based on a range of factors including potential for harm to the individual, potential for harm to society, and so on. LSD was ranked as an extremely low harm substance – especially in comparison to 'high harm' substances such as alcohol[1], ketamine and solvents.

Sadly, but perhaps not really surprisingly, Dr Nutt's findings were ignored by the government that they were presented to. Additionally though, after further work in the same direction, Dr Nutt was dismissed from his position on the advisory council. The Home Secretary, Alan Johnson, responsible for the dismissal wrote, "*He was asked to go because he can not be both a government adviser and a campaigner against government policy.*" This of course leads to the obvious question, what is the point of an advisory council if it is only allowed to agree with the present policy?

It is only fair to mention that other members of the government, including the Science Minister at the time – Lord Paul Drayson – were unhappy with the dismissal and considered it to have been improperly handled. But nevertheless, no offer was made for Dr Nutt to return to that position on the council and subsequent statements from Lord Drayson in a formal policy review confirmed that scientific advisors can be dismissed in such circumstances.

The problems caused by a lack of education are even further compounded by the media in the form of **miseducation**. They continue to 'educate' about LSD with negative examples only, never mentioning anything positive lest they be accused of 'pushing drugs' or similar.

---

[1] Yes, alcohol is a high-harm substance. Don't let the legal status fool you!

Balanced reporting on drugs of any kind is essentially non-existent. That is to say, you'll hear when someone who was using an illegal drug commits a crime, dies, or is otherwise in trouble; however, in the event that should someone discover or invent something when inspired by a psychedelic experience, the report of the discovery will almost certainly evade any mention of the substance.

The comedian Bill Hicks was well known for challenging the idea of 'accepted truth' and the negative slant that the media gives towards drugs. In many of his performances, he delivered a variant of the following to illustrate the point, "*Always that same LSD story, you've all seen it. 'Young man on acid, thought he could fly, jumped out of a building. What a tragedy.' What a dick! Fuck him, he's an idiot. If he thought he could fly, why didn't he take off on the ground first? You don't see ducks lined up to catch elevators to fly south — they fly from the ground. How about a positive LSD story? Wouldn't that be news-worthy, just the once? To base your decision on information rather than scare tactics and superstition and lies? I think it would be news-worthy. 'Today, a young man on acid realized that all matter is merely energy condensed to a slow vibration. That we are all one consciousness experiencing itself subjectively. There is no such thing as death, life is only a dream and we're the imagination of ourselves . . . Here's Tom with the weather.*" Wouldn't it be nice to hear that on the evening news, even just once?

Beyond the media, education campaigns in schools tend to suffer from the same problem. It is widely recognised that other similar abstinence campaigns – such as with sexual education – are far less effective than education that takes a more balanced and honest approach. I have yet to hear however of a drug education programme in place anywhere in the world that teaches anything beyond, *"drugs are bad; don't do drugs; if you do drugs, you're bad..."*

I certainly do not want to give the impression that I would endorse acceptance of children taking illegal substances – or even legal ones for that matter if the substances have psychoactive effects of even one one-hundredth of what LSD produces. I simply believe that if they are taught the real effects of different substances then perhaps when they are faced by the reality of drugs (as increasingly more children are in our society) they can make a more informed and reasoned decision to say no instead. The current scare tactics used in some places of trotting a meth-head out in front of the kids doesn't do much the first time they hear the truth that different drugs have different effects. Or, for those that do not hear that truth, they will grow up and shape the policies of tomorrow thinking the effects of all drugs – including LSD – are exactly the same as what they saw.

The current educational system is not only counter-productive, it is also horribly biased. They say, *"don't do drugs; and don't drink until you're older"*. Alcohol, as previously discussed in this book is a significantly more harmful and dangerous substance than many others and yet by virtue of an accident of history, it is commonly accepted in society whereas other substances are not. Again, the two possibilities are that children will realise the truth and then consider that *"since alcohol is dangerous, but still legal and acceptable, surely I can do anything else"*; or alternatively fail to realise the true dangers of alcohol and following their education assume that other substances are much worse. Neither of possible outcomes these are particular positive.

As it happens, we are not completely without any real world examples of legally available psychedelics. In the Netherlands, truffles (and mushrooms until quite recently) containing psilocybin are available for purchase in 'smart shops'. When purchasing them, the buyer is informed by the staff that they must not consume alcohol, marijuana (also available in the Netherlands) or any other drugs. A small pamphlet is then included with the purchase to give additional information that the user should read including links to websites that contain further information that the user might want to make themselves aware of if they choose to. In some locations – however unfortunately fewer than there used to be – there are 'chill out' lounges where people can consume their psilocybin and have their psychedelic experience in a relaxed and comfortable environment that is also safe and secure.

A similar situation for LSD should certainly be entirely possible; however, as the LSD experience can be much more powerful, profound and deeper than the psilocybin experience, perhaps additional safety measures could be taken. These could be for example the *requirement* that the user must stay in the 'chill out' lounge (which, for the best possible experience would also then have an enclosed outdoor area available) for the duration of the trip; that the information provided is more detailed; or that a particular process (involving education) must be followed to get a kind of card or other identification document that is then required when the user wishes to purchase LSD (and perhaps also other psychedelic substances).

These potential solutions to the question of legalisation would be acceptable from my point of view and I would welcome them as an extremely positive change in society.

Personally however, my preferred solution is somewhat more open still.

By now after reading this far, you may have come to the realisation that LSD is not for everyone. There are those who say it is too powerful an experience for anyone; there are others who have said it should be kept to specific 'classes' of people; and there are even those who have said that it should be given to everyone – whether they want it or not – in order to spread the idea of consciousness expansion amongst mankind.

It is true that not everyone can 'handle' an LSD experience and especially those that are unprepared. However, in my experience it is generally the case that people who take LSD when they are not correctly prepared for it will find the experience disturbing and unpleasant, and are therefore extremely unlikely to use it again after the first time – or if they do, will be better prepared for the experience. Furthermore, the type of people that either take a very small dose or combine it with MDMA and use it as a 'party drug' are certainly missing out on a great deal of the experience; but despite this aren't really causing any additional harm to themselves or others and so can also hardly be considered to be a problem. That mostly only leaves those who use it in a responsible manner and a very small number of people that might have problems.

Again using the Netherlands as a case study, it is apparent that more relaxed or open legislation does not lead to significantly increased consumption. Despite the ready availability of both marijuana and psilocybin in the Netherlands, the rates of use amongst people who live there are in fact on par with – or unexpectedly, in some cases a little lower than – many other western countries including neighbouring or nearby countries like Germany and France.

There is significant 'drug tourism' in the Netherlands due to the more relaxed laws for marijuana and psilocybin – especially in the city of Amsterdam – which would also be inevitable in any country that lessened the restrictions on LSD were they to do it first. However based on the experience of the Netherlands, this actually does not appear to be a particularly concerning issue either, as it brings in tourist money and does not appear to cause a significant public nuisance. The few times that something very bad has happened – such as a much publicised death by drowning in a canal after the consumption of magic mushrooms (combined with other substances, including alcohol) – it was an uncommon enough event to be widely reported both on television and in print media. Given the amount that tourists in Amsterdam use these substances (in the thousands to tens of thousands every day), this should give you an idea how rare such occurrences are in actuality.

I think it is safe to assume that if LSD were legalised in a manner similar to psilocybin truffles in the Netherlands (age limit; limited sales outlets; basic education at point of sale including printed material), there would be an initial spike in usage as some people decide to 'try it out', but only a slight increase in long term usage as people with the mind-set to benefit from it continue to use it but the 'novelty' has worn off for those who aren't ready for it. Overall, and in my opinion only, there would be no significant problems.

Regardless of which kind of legislation improvement would be chosen, any improvement would also of course greatly benefit researchers and therapists interested in LSD, as it would remove many of the legal barriers that presently exist for the substance.

Aside from the research discussed earlier in this book, there is one other kind of research that is not usually considered as such by the majority of people outside the world of psychedelics. That is the informal, non-medical, undocumented social experiment of those who believe or believed that LSD can 'change the world for the better'.

The theory goes that beyond the individual, society as a whole benefits from a populace that understands itself better. It is important to face negative aspects of the self and understand them so that improvement can occur in the individual, leading to a better society overall. However, many drugs – both prescription and recreational – are designed or used to numb anxiety, fear and existential distress, giving relief from the symptom, but doing nothing to help with the ailment.

These emotions are corrective mechanisms that tell us when we – or our society – are moving in the wrong direction. This points to a possible argument that the reason such 'numbing' drugs are becoming more of a problem in modern times is because our society is profoundly ill and we perceive that on some level. In the same way physical pain makes you pull your hand out of the fire, existential stress makes you re-evaluate your life and look at ways it could be made more meaningful and more fulfilling.

Instead, our current solution is to take drugs (whether prescription or not) to hide from our problems. To put it bluntly, why not just make a drug to cure ambition and sexual desire while we are at it and destroy the human race for good?

LSD will not numb these feelings; and may even bring them to the surface – this can be a powerful learning experience for the individual, which ultimately benefits the society as a whole given that enough people have had their consciousness and understanding of themselves expanded in this way.

There however is where we can say that the experiment has neither succeeded nor failed – the simple fact that it has not yet truly been performed. Even at the height of LSD use, the total percentage of the population of the world that had used it, or even the total percentage of the population of the countries in which it was most popular that had used it was still only a fraction of a percent.

Some days, I feel as if such an experiment would be a resounding success. Give LSD to everyone you can, teach them how to use it properly, and the world will be a much brighter and more wonderful place where the petty things that are argued over and fought for are seen to be as unimportant as they truly are. In the words of John Lennon's immortal song "Imagine": *"You may say I'm a dreamer, but I'm not the only one; I hope someday you'll join us; and the world will be as one."*

Other days, I am far less positive. Perhaps the majority aren't really ready for it. Consciousness expansion is not something that everyone can handle well – especially those that have spent their life avoiding learning anything outside of their narrow world-view. Maybe it would just lead to chaos. I really can not say for sure, nor do I think anyone else can.

So for now, it remains a thought experiment only.

The Chemistry

"I think that in human evolution it has never been as necessary to have this substance LSD. It is just a tool to turn us into what we are supposed to be."

Albert Hofmann

This chapter covers such topics as the chemical structure of LSD, the effects on brain chemistry, and a brief overview of how LSD is produced. It should not be considered a 'how to' guide for the production of LSD. As I have already mentioned, unless you are a chemist with access to specialist equipment, producing it is almost certainly well beyond your capabilities.

LSD is a relatively simple looking molecule, made up like most of the organic world out of Carbon, Hydrogen, Nitrogen and Oxygen. It can be written as $C_{20}H_{25}N_3O$.

This is a relatively fragile molecule and breaks down quite easily in to other substances. Oxygen, ultraviolet light and chlorine will all damage the LSD molecule; and the higher the temperature, the faster the LSD will be degraded.

LSD as a salt or a well-prepared solution can be kept stable essentially indefinitely if stored in a cool, dry, dark place in an airtight container. However, even with blotter tabs, careful storage will keep the LSD from degrading too significantly.

Personally, I used to keep blotter tabs stored in an airtight moisture proof bag, inside the pages of a book on a bookshelf in a room where the temperature neither rises particularly high nor drops particularly low. In these conditions, I have found the

LSD appears to remain stable for periods of at least up to six months with noticeable degradation after approximately one year, where it remains active, however at an approximate half-strength to when it was 'fresh'.

LSD production is notoriously difficult. There are two 'common' ways that it can be achieved. One is to begin with plants containing natural lysergic acid amine (LSA) such as the seeds of the morning glory flower; however this process is generally considered too impractical, expensive and difficult to perform without generating a large number of impurities.

The other – more 'standard' – method of production involves starting with the ergot fungus "*Claviceps Purpurea*" (relatively easy to find anywhere that wheat, rye or similar grains are grown); extracting ergotamine; performing alkaline hydrolysis to create lysergic acid; activating this with a reagent; and then finally reacting the activated lysergic acid with diethylamine. Many guides to the production can be found online and so a more detailed description is not warranted here.

A common myth about LSD tabs is that they are often 'adulterated' with strychnine – often using the statement that strychnine is somehow required to 'bind' LSD to the paper or that LSD naturally breaks down in to strychnine (both statements are completely untrue). Given that there is zero benefit for the seller to poison their customer and given that strychnine specifically would not fit on LSD blotter paper in any kind of active dose, this can quite clearly be marked off as nothing but a myth.

Another commonly held belief with no basis in reality is that LSD causes genetic mutations. A study performed in 1967 initially lent some credence to this myth, which has spurred the popularity since then. This study however was poorly conducted and controlled, and produced results that were as open to interpretation as the decision of the person using them. More strictly conducted and controlled experiments in 2008 refuted any possibility of chromosomal damage from LSD taken in normal doses. Another earlier study in 1969 showed there may even be a slight effect of improved chromosomal reproduction – that is, *less* genetic mutations – in the presence of LSD, however to be fair, these results may also have been a matter of interpretation more than anything as with the more negative 1967 study.

Yet a third myth is that LSD is not removed from the body and remains within you forever after taking it. This myth is used to attempt to explain flashbacks, but yet again has no basis in reality. The most common place mentioned is spinal fluid, which is also the place many other drugs that supposedly stay in your system forever are said to end up. The second most commonly stated variant is that it remains in your fat, and flashbacks are caused when the fat is broken down as you lose weight. The reality is that LSD is broken down by the liver in around five hours (less time than the length of the trip itself) and could not possibly be stored in fat as it is fat insoluble.

Not everything said about LSD is a myth however – despite the large amount of untrue statements that are regularly made, occasionally some truth slips through in the mix.

One such truth is that not all LSD is equally as pure. This is especially true for LSD procured from an unknown or unreliable source. As previously discussed, it is extraordinarily unlikely that it has been deliberately adulterated in any way – and especially not with strychnine as stated – but that does not mean it is chemically pure.

The process of creating LSD is difficult. There are many different chemicals used and even the 'end product' goes through more than one chemical state before it is finally converted to LSD. If the process is not followed precisely, there can be leftover traces of either the reagents[1] or precursors[2].

Chemically impure LSD therefore can potentially contain trace amounts of clavine alkaloids, unhydrolysed ergot alkaloids, unreacted lysergic acid, lysergic acid hydrazides, or a range of solvents that were used during the process.

Beyond the reagents and precursors, LSD production can also produce other substances besides LSD when the process is not correctly followed.

Commonly, an isomer of LSD called 'iso-LSD' is created. Iso-LSD has no psychoactive effects and a good chemist will convert any iso-LSD created in to LSD. If it is left in the mix, it simply means that the LSD will be proportionally weaker than it should be for the same quantity.

Additionally, if the person creating the LSD does not have access to the right equipment, it is likely they will create the LSD in normal air instead of a pure nitrogen atmosphere. This causes the LSD to begin decaying *very* rapidly until it is stabilised by putting it in solution. Therefore, many of the decay chemicals of LSD may also be present in a typical batch that was produced in a 'back-room' environment rather than a professional lab.

---

[1] Chemicals used to create reactions.

[2] Chemicals that were to be converted to LSD but were not.

It is important to reiterate, as mentioned earlier in this book, that chemically impure LSD however is very unlikely to have a different effect than chemically pure LSD does. The reason for this is simple quantities – as discussed, LSD active dosages are an order of magnitude or more lower than active dosages of almost all other chemicals. Therefore, even if fifty percent of the crystal substance that was assumed to be LSD is in fact something else, what you are getting is a half-strength dose of LSD plus a tiny amount of something else that will have little to no effect of any kind.

Michael Valentine Smith clarified this in his book "*Psychedelic Chemistry*" by saying, "*There is a great deal of superstition regarding purification of psychedelics. Actually, any impurities which may be present as a result of synthetic procedures will almost certainly be without any effect on the trip.*

If there are 200 micrograms of impurities present... and few compounds will produce a significant effect until a hundred to a thousand times this amount has been ingested. Even mescaline, which has a rather specific psychedelic effect, requires about a thousand times this amount."

This line of thinking has been argued against, in that if you have something which is 'very similar to LSD, but not LSD', it may bind to the same receptors in the brain, effectively blocking the LSD from doing so, or performing a similar function but in a manner that is different and possibly less pleasant – essentially 'bad acid'.

These arguments however seem to be based around the idea that it is not known where and how LSD binds within the brain. One such statement based on a random statement made in an opinion piece written in 1977 covering the same argument even considers the brain stem as a binding position – not a terrible assumption given the state of knowledge in 1977, but very clearly not true according to current research and knowledge.

Also, if it were the case, then it would be reasonably expected that these substances when *not* in the presence of LSD would also have powerful psychoactive effects. Yet no reagent, precursor or even isomer of LSD (that may be produced accidentally in the process) are shown to have any such psychoactive effect at all at the dosages that LSD is taken in.

There are substances with similar workings to LSD, which are chemically very similar. As an example, ALD-52 (N-acetyl-LSD) produces very similar effects to LSD at around ninety percent of the potency according to the majority of reports. ALD-52 could conceivably be produced when LSD was intended to be produced, but as (depending on the method of production) it is generally an *additional* step rather than a failure to perform a step correctly, it is unlikely that a manufacturer would produce this substance by mistake.

Much of the arguments about 'low quality' LSD are from subjective experience. Ken Kesey for example claimed that the 'pure LSD' he got from the government as he was participating in trials was significantly better than what was available on the 'streets' some time later and attributed this to the purity of the substance. Perhaps a better theory as to why the experience was subjectively different was his own expectations and experiences interfering with or clouding his judgement in addition to the actual quantity of LSD on the 'street acid' being lower than advertised or expected.

I can also personally quite definitely say that my first ever LSD experience – while significantly more horrific than later experiences – was a much more profound and deep experience, quite simply because it was something totally new to me and a truly shocking experience. There is no reason to assume that my first LSD was any more chemically pure than the LSD I had later. This is especially true as I once had the opportunity to take 'very pure' LSD produced for a medical trial (and 'redirected' outside of the trial) and can not say – subjectively or objectively – that the experience was truly any different to approximately the same quantity of LSD from a less 'reputable' source.

It is possible of course that thirty five years ago when the aforementioned opinion piece was written, that the availability of chemically pure LSD was significantly lower or that somehow other substances were more common and being sold as if they were LSD, however today there is no evidence for that continuing to be the case. Perhaps because the popularity has declined, the remaining manufacturers are now more serious about the substance than when demand was high enough that 'getting it out the door' was the highest priority; or perhaps it was never a problem and the opinion piece was simply wrong. Regardless of the situation *then*, the situation *now* is that all LSD I have ever procured has only varied in strength, and not in subjective 'quality of trip'. The only time I have had subjectively different trips where when I was taking something that was not LSD at all – psilocybin, mescaline, and so on.

When LSD decomposes, the most common decomposition is to a substance called 'lumi-LSD', which is quite simply LSD that is saturated with water. Another possible substance is 'iso-LSD', which as mentioned above is also often produced during the production of LSD.

Lumi-LSD has no psychoactive properties or indeed any other effect on humans at all in doses of up to ten milligrams (fifty to one hundred times a typical LSD dosage). It is unknown if higher doses may have an effect, but given you are unlikely to deliberately consume ten milligrams of LSD, it seems fairly irrelevant if even a significant percentage of it were this inactive compound.

As with any chemical, The LSD molecule or 'parts of it' can be considered to be in a particular 'family' of substances. When talking about psychedelics, the vast majority are tryptamines – such as psilocybin and DMT – or have the 'important' part of the tryptamine structure in their molecular makeup. This 'important part' in this context is the 'indole ring' and is present on LSD, as well as substances such as ibogaine and yohimbine.

Not all tryptamines produce psychedelic effects. In fact, your brain relies on a particular tryptamine – serotonin – as a neurotransmitter that plays a vital role in your daily life. No matter how much serotonin you consume, you will never get a psychedelic effect (if you were to consume too much, you would however suffer 'serotonin shock' and likely die).

Looking at the chemical structures of these substances, the similarity should be startlingly clear, even to a non-chemist.

LSD   Serotonin   Psilocybin

If you do not see it immediately, take note of the structure at the bottom of all three figures, with the hexagon and pentagon structures where the pentagon has $\overset{N}{H}$ at the lower right corner.

These two structures together make up the aforementioned 'indole ring'.

At times, you may wish to test if a particular substance you have in your possession is LSD. Testing an unknown substance to determine what it is can be a complex chemical process, however there are some things you can do to at least determine if the substance is 'likely' to be LSD.

As mentioned in an earlier chapter, pure LSD will fluoresce (glow) blue or bluish-white under an ultraviolet light. This is most noticeable with LSD in a liquid form, however may also be seen on blotter paper or other forms.

There are three things that can complicate this however.

Firstly, that many inks used on blotter paper will also fluoresce (including possibly the same colour). This is usually noticeable however, as if the ink fluoresces, you can expect a much brighter fluorescence than you would expect if only the small amount of LSD on the blotter were doing so.

The second complication is that the quantity of LSD on blotter is very small and so only a very low amount of fluorescence may be seen, even in a dark room – possibly none at all in tabs of less than 100µg or so.

The third complication is that quite recently (from around 2010 onwards) there are some other psychedelic substances sold on blotter paper (specifically 25I-NBOMe and 25C-NBOMe are common) that also fluoresce in a similar way. With these substances however, the colour of the fluorescence tends more towards pink or orange and so should be easy to distinguish.

A chemical test is much more reliable, however likely also much more difficult to get your hands on the appropriate testing materials (compared to a UV light anyway). Home testing kits can be purchased from a variety of sources and are not illegal in most jurisdictions. That said however, you may want to be cautious if you live in a place where ordering this kind of equipment might cause you to end up on a watch list for 'suspicious activity' or so.

The standard chemical test is called 'Ehrlich's reagent test' where p–dimethylaminobenzaldehyde (most commonly simply called "DMAB") dissolved in an ethanol and hydrochloric acid mix will cause a reaction with substances that have an indole ring as described above (therefore including LSD), making the test liquid change colour to a shade of pink through to purple. Variants of the test use phosphoric acid and methanol; however, the principle of the test's action is the same.

Obviously, this test will also show positive for other substances that also have an indole ring, but generally, the quantity of the substance should also be an indicator, as most psychedelics that have an indole ring require a significantly larger dose.

Now that we roughly know what LSD is from a chemical perspective, the next question for us to address is how it works within the brain when it is taken.

When LSD is ingested or otherwise put in to the bloodstream, it passes the blood/brain barrier and begins to take effect.

The mechanism of action is extremely complex and due to our somewhat limited understanding of the functioning of the human brain, we can not precisely say what it is that makes LSD do what it does.

While our understanding of the brain is limited, it is by no means completely absent and we can describe quite well, at least on a superficial level, what LSD does inside the brain.

The brain contains receptors that in the presence of different chemical substances will be either activated/stimulated (agonistic effect) or deactivated/dampened (antagonistic effect). These receptors are generally affected by the brain's own chemistry. Specifically, the neurotransmitters adrenaline[1], noradrenaline[2], dopamine, melatonin[3] and serotonin play large roles.

Adrenaline and noradrenaline play a large role in movement, basic body regulation through muscle control (both voluntary and involuntary, such as the heart and blood vessels) and sugar/fat conversions.

Dopamine plays a role in a variety of tasks and concepts in the brain including cognition, motivation, punishment and reward, memory and learning, as well as being vital for sleep and dreaming. The most well known role of dopamine is that in the reward pathways of the brain. When you 'feel good' about completing a task or doing well in something, this is a direct

---

[1] Also called epinephrine

[2] Similarly, also called norepinephrine

[3] Not to be confused with 'melanin' which is a completely different substance and is responsible for skin and hair colouration.

result of higher levels of dopamine, and leads to a desire to repeat the experience – in a way, this is a kind of biological 'internal addiction' and is responsible for most kinds of psychological addiction as discussed in an earlier chapter. Overly high levels of dopamine however are associated with low-empathy, risk-taking behaviour, and may also be associated with certain kinds of psychosis.

Melatonin is best known as the hormone that helps manage your natural sleep/wake cycles. It is a tryptamine, like serotonin and LSD. Beyond managing your 'natural clock', it may have roles to play in mood, thermoregulation (controlling your body's temperature) and immunomodulation (managing aspects of your immune system). Some of these may be secondary effects to the management of your natural clock however, as mood, temperature and immune system management are all linked closely to sleep/wake cycles in general.

Serotonin (chemically knows as 5-hydroxytryptamine or simply '5-HT') is a very interesting neurotransmitter. As mentioned above, it is a tryptamine, however does not produce psychedelic effects in and of itself. It has an effect that touches almost all aspects of human behaviour. It has direct influence on appetite, understanding of social situations, and some automatic functions such as breathing and heartbeat control. Moreover, it seems it is a general regulatory control neurotransmitter than allows for finer, subtler interaction with your environment, most especially including interaction with other people. Relatedly, it also manages many aspect of mood, which is why anti-depressant drugs generally target the 5-HT receptors – or at least a subset of them – in some way.

Psilocybin (found in 'magic mushrooms') is a psychedelic substance – yet another tryptamine – with a similar, but not identical, effect on the mind to LSD. Psilocybin works mostly on the serotonin receptors of the brain due to the similar structure allowing it to bind to these receptors easily. LSD also heavily affects these receptors, for much the same reason, and so it seems extremely likely that this is the cause of the similar effects.

The serotonin receptors subtypes activated by psychedelics like psilocybin are quite limited in number compared to other kinds of receptors and are condensed mainly in one area of the brain. Despite the narrow scope of the area, these receptors have a modulating effect on almost every action in the brain due to a wide distribution of axons – a kind of nerve ending in a way – that maps to almost the entire of the rest of the brain.

In contrast to psilocybin however, LSD works on more than twenty receptors and sub-receptors within the brain and so the effects are more wide reaching and even more difficult to map.

It is also worth noting that these receptors are only a small part of the story. Knowing which receptors are activated tells you what is happening on top, as looking at both the front and back cover of a book will give you some ideas about the book. The cascade effects from this however are what truly matters and this is a much more complex topic that is unfortunately not well understood or easy to analyse in a living, functioning human brain.

Neuroimaging studies performed with the psychedelic substances psilocybin and DMT have shown that under the influence of psychedelic substances there is 'more' happening than there is without psychedelics. Sadly, to date, it seems no studies have been performed with LSD directly; however, the results from psilocybin and DMT should be considered at the very least an indicator of what could be expected with LSD as well.

In these studies, it was shown that the frontal areas of the brain – where dopamine plays the dominant role as a neurotransmitter – show a little more activation. The occipital lobe – where vision is managed – also shows some additional activation. The temporal lobe – where visual memories, language comprehension, emotion, and derivation of meaning are managed – shows some additional activation as well.

However, the primary effect shown by the imaging studies is in the limbic system.

The limbic system is also sometimes called the *paleomammalian brain* and forms a kind of core on which the rest of the brain is built around. You can crudely think of it as being a more basic kind of simple brain that was used in our primitive ancestors millions of years ago. It formed around the even simpler 'lizard brain', which corresponds to the human brain stem and the deepest structures connected to it, and then the complex modern mammalian brain grew around and expanded upon it (this really isn't the most accurate of descriptions from a scientific viewpoint, but it serves our purposes here).

The purpose of the limbic system is to manage some core functions between other brain areas, as well as controlling many of the more 'base' parts of the mind. Your 'fight or flight' response, 'gut feelings', base emotions, and so on are all centred here. This is the reason that LSD makes you 'feel more', especially with regards to your deeper, more 'inner' self.

As described right near the start of the first chapter in this book, sensory input comes from your sensory organs to your brain's thalamus. Under normal circumstances, information is then taken from the frontal cortex to apply a 'concept' to this sensory data. And – as described – LSD hinders this communication.

The thalamus seems to be responsible for both processing and relaying of sensory information (with the notable exception of the sense of smell). These general functions are not disrupted by LSD, however parts of them may be heightened significantly to an 'overloaded' state, which could well be the cause of the sensory distortions experienced during a trip.

What is disrupted by LSD is what happens after the thalamus receives and processes this data. It is not entirely clear in what way the communication with the 'conceptual data' in the frontal cortex is handled as the thalamus has an astounding number of connections to other areas of the brain, acting as a kind of 'switchboard' of information regarding sensory input. For example, it sends information received from the eyes to the occipital lobe, but also receives data back from the occipital lobe regarding this sensory data in a modified state before it then makes use of the communication path to the frontal cortex.

With this connection to the frontal cortex either weakened or removed, the information is instead stored directly to the hippocampus where it can then be stored as a memory and accessed by the conscious mind. The conscious mind is also located in the frontal cortex for the most part; however the opportunity for automatic 'application of concept' has now passed and you are aware of the sensory information without this having happened.

It is important to note that all of the descriptions provided here are simplified only. The brain is an extraordinarily complex thing and we are only beginning to understand some of the ways in which it functions. If you are interested in learning more about the brain, there are many good books on the subject (including some specifically about the pharmacology of LSD) which will explain in much greater depth and accuracy the topics that I have only brushed over here in this chapter.

Final Words

*"Don't take LSD unless you are very well prepared,
unless you are specifically prepared to go out of your
mind. Don't take it unless you have someone that's
very experienced with you to guide you through it. And
don't take it unless you are ready to have your
perspective on yourself and your life radically changed,
because you're gonna be a different person, and you
should be ready to face this possibility."*

Timothy Leary

In the pages of this book, you've read about the effects that LSD has on a mind; what you can roughly expect for your first trip; how a trip generally progresses from the start through to the end; some stories of first trips that were taken; dangers, risks and panic; self-discovery and creativity; research, medicine, history and law; and the chemical and biological workings of this substance.

LSD is a substance that has a powerful effect on the mind – one that is not to be underestimated. It produces a profoundly changed state of mind that allows you to examine your inner self in ways that you might never otherwise be able to do. Taking it can be a beautiful and marvellous experience, or it can be truly horrific if you are unprepared.

Hopefully, throughout this book you have learned many new and interesting things that you did not previously know; and I also hope that you now have a greater understanding of – and respect for – this very incredible substance and the states of mind that it produces.

If I have succeeded in doing what I set out to do, you now have a better idea of the effects of LSD and if you choose to try it yourself, you are better prepared for the experience than you would otherwise have been.

No matter how long I made this book however, there would be no way I could tell you 'everything there is to know' and thus I have glossed over some things where perhaps you wanted to know more.

The best way to learn more about the subject at this point is of course to have an LSD experience for yourself. If you are interested in doing so, but feel there are some important things that I have not covered however, you are both invited and encouraged to investigate and read further yourself. There is a wealth of resources available to you if you are interested in learning more about any of the things that I have covered in this book.

One of the most valuable resources for information about any recreational drug is 'Erowid'. Erowid is a foundation that runs a website at *http://www.erowid.org* – here, you will find fair, balanced and unbiased data about chemical information; research papers; books; thousands of personal accounts; and much more on almost any recreational drug you can think of (and very many you've probably never heard of before).

Another useful resource is your friendly online encyclopædia – Wikipedia. Wikipedia is not always reliable in and of itself, being editable by anyone means that false information can and does occasionally creep in (although on many – if not most – articles, most incorrect information is quickly reverted by those who have taken an interest in maintaining the article). However, what is perhaps most useful is that good information is always referenced, with links to the original source. Reading articles on Wikipedia will give you a good further overview of many of the topics in this book, with references to the source material if you want to read further or fact-check the information that you find there.

Yet another online destination that can be useful is 'bluelight' – a discussion forum website at *http://www.bluelight.ru* – the forums on this site contain discussion about a wide range of recreational substances, including of course LSD. Be aware however that as a site where really anyone can write whatever he or she wants, you are likely to come across a wealth of misinformation here in amongst the accurate information.

There are also of course many other books that I read while writing this one. Some present a different viewpoint to mine, some similar. Most contain a similar range of topics to this book, but with a different focus or emphasis. Others focus on specific aspects in much greater detail while leaving out the more general information. Many are sadly very out of date and information that I have regarding research, medicine and the law is probably more current than most (at least as of September 2013).

I can also highly recommend a small number of very interesting documentaries. A lot have been made over the years, including a large number with a decidedly negative spin as explained in this book. However there are some that are more unbiased (and of course some biased towards LSD) that I would definitely suggest as being useful and interesting to watch.

Without further ado, here are my recommendations:

Books:

- LSD: My Problem Child; Albert Hofmann
- The Pharmacology of LSD: A critical review; Annelie Hintzen & Torsten Passie
- TiHKAL (Tryptamines i Have Known And Loved); Alexander & Ann Shulgin
- The Doors of Perception; Aldous Huxley
- LSD, the Problem Solving Psychedelic; Peter G. Stafford

Documentaries:

- The Substance: Albert Hoffman's LSD
- Magic Trip
- Ecstasy Bandits
- LSD: The Beyond Within

Web:

- http://www.erowid.org/chemicals/lsd/
- http://en.wikipedia.org/wiki/Lysergic_acid_diethylamide
- http://en.wikipedia.org/wiki/History_of_lysergic_acid_diethylamide
- http://en.wikipedia.org/wiki/Psychedelics_in_problem-solving_experiment
- http://en.wikipedia.org/wiki/List_of_misconceptions_about_illegal_drugs#LSD
- http://www.thelancet.com/journals/lancet/article/PIIS0140-6736(07)60464-4/
- http://www.maps.org
- http://www.bluelight.ru
- and of course: http://www.google.com/search?q=lsd

You are also welcome to contact me directly via email. My email address is:

dalebewan@gmail.com

You can also join others that have read this book in discussion or talk directly with me at this book's facebook page:

http://www.facebook.com/DroppingAcidDaleBewan

Please note that I am not able to respond to all mail that I receive, however if your email asks a question and is sincere, I will do my best to respond. Hopefully understandably, I **can not** and **will not** respond to requests on further information for where to purchase LSD (or any other illegal substance) or requests that ask me to provide it for you.

Printed in Great Britain
by Amazon